Editor
Walter Kelly, M.A.

Managing Editor
Ina Massler Levin, M.A.

Cover Artist
Barb Lorseyedi

Art Manager
Kevin Barnes

Art Director
CJae Froshay

Imaging
Rosa C. See

Publisher
Mary D. Smith, M.S. Ed.

How to Manage an
Independent Reading Program

Grades 4–8

Author

Irene Parisi, M.S.

Teacher Created Resources, Inc.
6421 Industry Way
Westminster, CA 92683
www.teachercreated.com

ISBN-1-4206-3125-X

©2005 Teacher Created Resources, Inc.

Made in U.S.A.

Teacher Created Resources

Table of Contents

Introduction

In a typical year, a teacher can anticipate at least four reading groups, all of which may be at different reading levels. This means that teachers have to expect students to work independently for at least a two-and-a-half-hour block. While teachers meet with groups, those in-group students are assured of a quality reciprocal model lesson using the four good-reader strategies: (1) clarify, (2) predict, (3) question, and (4) summarize. The challenge has always been for those students who are not in-group. Ideally, these students would be engaged in centers with well-designed activities that prompt the use of the same good-reader strategies that connect to what is being taught in the classroom. For teachers, therefore, the dilemma (and the challenge) seems to be *"What do I do with my other students when I am working with reading groups? How do I provide thoughtful, meaningful, independent activities?"*

Teachers struggle with these questions and work late to provide every student with such high-quality, meaningful activities. Following discussion with colleagues and interaction at professional development opportunities, teachers may recognize as commonplace the following problems:

1. Not enough student response to authentic text in the classroom.
2. Not enough opportunity for the students to self-select a text they want to read.
3. Not enough activities to actively engage students in the process of thoughtful, meaningful reading.

Ultimately, research and revisiting the state content and standards aligned with the curriculum will help to create a classroom structure that addresses these problems. From just such research, this independent reading program was created. This program encourages the use of the following reciprocal reading strategies:

- Clarifying
- Predicting
- Questioning
- Summarizing

This instructional program is very effective in helping below-level readers accelerate their reading by using these four reading strategies for constructing meaning.

The program also encourages the use of the **QAR** (*Question, Answer, Response/Relationship*) **Model,** as researched and shared by Taffy Raphael. **QAR** is a reading strategy used by students to help them categorize comprehension questions according to where they found the information they needed to answer each question. Students actively share whether their answers were (1) *textually explicit*, (2) *textually implicit*, or (3) *created entirely from the students' own background knowledge*.

Introduction *(cont.)*

The next step this program encourages is revisiting respective state-mandated standardized-testing strands and objectives. In general, most such strands and objectives reveal that when reading, students are expected to do the following:

- *apply initial understanding*
- *develop interpretations*
- *move beyond the text and form a critical stance by analyzing author's purpose and craft*
- *form an opinion on what they have read.*

The final step to ensure this program's success is for teachers to look for what is lacking in the current independent activities being provided within the classroom. Once teachers have ascertained this, they can implement the program, which is a *self-managing, daily reading-response activity based on students self-selecting the text and critically analyzing and connecting to it.*

By creating and organizing a monthly calendar of responses, teacher will have 25 days of lessons compiled on the first day of the month. Teachers will have additional opportunities to use the response activities as meaningful mini-lessons aligned with a specific strand or objective that can be delivered prior to group or independent work. Each response takes approximately 15–20 minutes to complete. Students tend to look forward to these activities of 15–20 minutes duration. Since the response activity is not time-consuming and students are selecting texts at their comfort level, every student can be successful. This is an activity that teachers can count on being completed each day with quality. Teachers are encouraged to create a title to use for this program in the classroom. Here are some examples:

- "Take the Lead and Read"
- "Quality Reading Time"
- "Read and Succeed"

Choose one of these or create one of your own that will appeal to your students. And whatever you choose to call this block of time or program, it will work because students are self-selecting at their comfort level and continually reading familiar text. In doing so, they are increasing their fluency and their ability to analyze a text in multiple ways.

What teachers will find in this book is an organized approach to providing meaningful independent activities while other groups are meeting. Teachers will find the independent activities have strong connections to what is already being done in the classroom, thus reinforcing what is being taught in the reading groups. Teachers will also find that if a leap of faith is taken in our students' abilities to work independently, they can succeed. High expectations breed high success!

What Is This Independent Reading Program All About?

This book describes how to manage a classroom reading program that fosters self-selection of a text by the students, followed by activities using the reciprocal reading strategies of Clarify, Predict, Question, and Summarize. (*An overview of this strategy and mini-lessons can be found in Chapter 5, page 11 and Chapter 7, pages 15–36.*)

Monthly Calendars

Students will manage their independent reading by following a monthly calendar designed by the teacher. The calendar will describe each daily activity for a four-week period. Monthly calendars may be created to accompany a given type of text, such as with summer reading. The teacher may create the form by using software such as *Appleworks Calendar Assistant* or other calendar creator programs. Also, *Microsoft Word* can be used by inserting tables and then adding the response activities. A year's set of calendar reproducibles (complete with activities) can be found in Chapter 8 (pages 37–63). Teachers are free to use the activities in the calendars as they are presented here, add to them, delete them, or otherwise amend them to best fit individual needs.

Daily Reading Response

Each day's independent learning is designed as a response activity that can relate to any text the student selects. The response activity will foster independent reading within the classroom during an independent work period. Responses, of course, can be designed to relate to current classroom themes or holidays and occasions.

Reading Response Journals

After students have selected a text from the classroom library, they are to respond to the open-ended questions in their calendars, and then place their responses in a journal provided by the teacher. The journal is best kept in a specific independent reading folder. The entire folder is to be handed in for review during the language arts block.

Activities

Activities will focus on having students create higher-order questions from the text, as well as answering open-ended, higher-order thinking questions. Each activity takes no more than 15–20 minutes each day to complete. As the year progresses, responses can become more involved and encompass a larger scope of work. Many of the question stems and responses found in this book are generic; however, they are thoughtful questions that align with the research of QAR and higher-order thinking.

> This program provides the teacher with a powerful method of managing group instruction that fosters independent reading of a quality type—one clearly aligned with developing higher-order thinking skills and leading to strong individual competence.

What Is This Independent Reading Program All About? *(cont.)*

Benefits Afforded by This Independent Reading Program

- Students will increase their independent reading time for 170 days in a year.

- Students will increase their connection to any given text.

- Students will select books at their comfort level and take ownership in their responses.

- Students will increase their use and understanding of the reciprocal reading strategies while reading all genres of literature.

- Students will improve their ability to respond to a given text in a higher order manner.

- ESOL students and emergent readers will increase opportunities to read at their comfort level.

- Classroom learners will share their reading experiences in reading groups with a personal connection.

- Students will improve their sense of responsibility in managing independent work time.

- Every student will engage in reading independently.

- Students will have increased opportunities for partner reading experiences.

- Students will increase their exposure to nonfiction texts, and thus to higher order knowledge.

- Students will enjoy their time spent reading.

Assessment

This independent reading program also provides the teacher with an alternative tool of assessment. Folders may be collected on a daily, weekly, or monthly basis to review the types of responses students are creating. The folders and journals may be used for conferences between students and teacher, teacher and parent, and student to student. Additional ideas on how to assess this program can be found in Chapter 9 (page 64).

Setting Up the Program

Step One

First, obtain a basic file folder for each student. It is wise to prepare each folder with a sticker bearing the program name on the front—for example, "Take the Lead and READ." Then place a grading sticker on the back of the folder. These can be made on the computer by running label paper through the printer. Inside the folder, the teacher should place a blue-book journal and copies of the reading log, sentence stems, and bookmarks. Sticker and folder contents can be found in Chapter 10 (pages 65–80) as reproducibles.

Step Two

Second, organize the classroom library by genre (*make sure to review this word with the students, as it will be used often in discussing books they are reading*). An overview of setting up an effective classroom library can be found in Chapter 3 (page 8). Within the classroom library, make space for two cardboard magazine holders to hold students' independent reading response folders. These may be purchased from any office supply store. This area will become the "reading response" area throughout the year. Students will know where to find the folders each day and become responsible for getting their folders during the independent work time. However, students should hand the folders in for review in the language arts bin each day. Methods of assessing can be found in Chapter 9 (page 64).

Step Three

Next, prepare the calendar for the month. This monthly calendar ensures that there is a daily activity that each learner can respond to. Teachers generally have an idea two to four weeks in advance what they will be working on, such as themes or units in all disciplines (including science and social studies) that they can incorporate into the calendar. Once the calendar has been reviewed, students keep it in their folders, and the teacher can post a master copy in a designated area, such as a bulletin board in the library.

A one-year gathering of calendars with activities can be found in Chapter 8 (pages 37–63). The QAR model (page 28) and standardized testing strands and objectives can help build open-ended responses that can be used for any selected text. If the calendar activities included in this book do not support a specific month within your curriculum, a blank 25-day calendar is included for your specific creation.

Step Four

Finally, begin the first weeks of school modeling for the students (1) how to select an appropriate text, (2) how to effectively respond to text, (3) how to use the good reader strategies of *clarify*, *predict*, *question*, and *summarize*, (4) how to choose a graphic organizer, and (5) how to assess themselves based on the standardized three-point open-ended response rubric. A few days spent practicing the program is useful—even working on noise level (asking for help or clarification) and what to do when finished.

Once everyone is confident and groups have been organized, the program is up and running.

Creating the Classroom Library

Heart of the Classroom

There is no definitive way to set up a classroom library; one should, however, strive to make it inviting to students. Create a space that encourages students to browse, touch, examine, talk, read, react, sit, and write. Make this area the heart of the classroom. Not only should books be in this area, but also pens, pencils, paper, sticky notes, and questioning-the-text bookmarks (see pages 71–73 for samples). This sort of environment encourages easy and automatic response to what has been read.

Organization

An effective classroom library is one that is organized and kept user-friendly. Using familiar sections like those found in the local library or bookstore is helpful. Sectioning and labeling shelves by genre will enable students to browse these sections with an understanding that the book they are scanning or reading is strictly fiction, nonfiction, biography, science, and so on. Browsing boxes and baskets are also helpful in any classroom library. These can be designed by level or theme.

Maintenance

In order to maintain organization and care of books, encourage students to report any damaged books so that they may be repaired and quickly returned to the library. This practice promotes respect for what is being read. Try to limit the use of tattered and torn books in the library.

Location

A classroom library situated in a corner away from heavy traffic is helpful. A library in the front of the classroom can give the impression that books are important, but classroom libraries have been effective in the back corner of the room as well. An open area with a rug or furniture adds an inviting and safe appeal to the students. Low-level lighting, such as clip-on lamps or library table lamps, adds an ambience that students appreciate. Within a library with lamp, book, paper, and pen, students tend to create a comfortable space they enjoy revisiting each day.

Book Boxes

To help traffic flow in the library and to build confidence when selecting a text, each student can create a personal book box. On the first day of school, instruct students to bring an empty cereal box to class. Once all students have boxes, show them how to construct a personal book box in which they are to store all their self-selected books. Model how to cut one corner of the box on a diagonal, thus creating a magazine-type holder. Next, provide each student with special paper (shiny or thematic). Model how to wrap the book box. Send each box home with students, accompanied by a letter encouraging parents to help their students decorate the box so that it is special to them and illustrates a love for reading and books. Students should return the next day with the completed boxes.

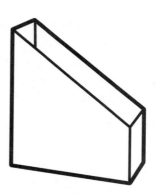

Chapter 3

Creating the Classroom Library *(cont.)*

Contents

Ideally, the contents of a classroom library will include a wide range and variety of text, reading level, and genre: fiction, nonfiction, science, social studies, biography, etc. Teachers should take advantage of the rich selection of fiction that can be assembled from lists of Newbery Medal winners, for example, along with other selections from appropriate sources. Although a classroom library may start out relatively small, it can be enriched and expanded periodically with funds from the school's classroom budget along with donations from such groups as the P.T.A. or other parent associations.

Selection

Using a teacher sample, deliver a mini-lesson on distinguishing among the various genres and demonstrating how to select texts. Provide time for students to fill their book boxes with self-selected texts at the close of the lesson. Encourage students to keep these selected books for at least a week. Some students, depending on interest level, may choose to keep their books for a month. When students are directed to work on independent reading responses, encourage them to search their book boxes for an appropriate text to use.

Encourage book swapping if one student happens to have a book another student wants to read. If the classroom library is small, this strategy is very useful. When book boxes are not in use, store them within the classroom library. These book boxes are natural resources—also known as "lifesavers"— when there are early finishers during other activities, transitions, D.E.A.R. time (*Drop Everything and Read*), or after testing situations.

Goal

The goal of your classroom library is to invite students into the process of reading and response. An independent reading program of necessity requires a library—one that is immediately accessible and inviting. In fact, the library should become a magnet that draws students into its magical circle and becomes the students' natural habitat—a place for learning, exploring, and expressing (or responding). Remember that an independent reading program such as the one developed in this book depends on the critical relationship between reading and response. That is why the library is not just a passive area—a place to sit and look at books as one would a TV program. The library should become vital, interactive—even dynamic—in the sense that each student should engage in individual growth through expanding levels of open-ended questions leading to higher-level thinking. When the student is offered daily individual experience in such activity, the natural outcome is a student who grows in confidence and competence, one who not only acquires knowledge but who also gains powerful higher-order thinking skills.

Chapter 4

Responding to Text

Reading and response (that is, reading and then directly responding to that reading) is a practice that is needed daily in any grade. The levels of response should naturally advance and expand with age and exposure to authentic text and increased reading experiences. The rationale of this program supports the idea that students will be assessed on their answers (responses) through the use of a standardized testing/scoring rubric.

It stands to reason that if students are going to be assessed, then they should know *how* they are being assessed and *what* they are being assessed on. Following this reasoning, you should make a basic scoring rubric available to the students early in the year so that there are no surprises. In the beginning of the year, provide many lessons with the whole group responding to text activities that can be assessed by student peers. Allow opportunities for students to discuss why an answer may be assessed as a "1," a "2," or a "0." This method of introducing a scoring rubric such as the one below and analyzing it in "kid-friendly" terms helps to set expectations for a response.

	Open-Ended Response Scoring Rubric*
2	Response presents a reasonable explanation that answers the question. Response uses specific, relevant details from the passage as support.
1	Response presents a mostly reasonable explanation that answers the question. Response uses general information as support, rather than details from the passage.
0	Response presents an unreasonable explanation that does not answer the question. The response is vague.

*Rubric developed by the National Assessment Governing Board Reading Framework for the National Assessment of Educational Progress.

Begin by reviewing and clarifying specific words students may not know. Connect to personal experiences when reviewing the word *vague* (concrete personal examples are often needed to clarify the meaning of this word). For example, people often ask for something without saying what the "something" is. ("Would you bring me that *thing* over on the *whatchamacallit*?") Students will laugh and share their connections. Allow this to happen as it will bring to life the meaning of the "vague" response. As the understanding of vagueness is shared as well as personal experiences of "vagueness," the fear of not understanding the scoring rubric subsides.

By the lesson's end, students will know that they are expected to complete each response with quality, as outlined in their rubric. Over time, students will begin to grade themselves and each other, using this rubric. Again, it is important that students see what they are being graded on and how. It should be no secret to them. Through modeling open-ended responses, students can explore what kinds of responses are acceptable at their level. It can also be very effective for the teacher to relate the responses to any real world situation.

After a few days of having the whole group respond to text activities, students can be introduced to this independent reading program. The group responses, which were designed to give the students practice and confidence, will now, of course, become the basis for individual and independent responses as the students move ahead on their own.

The Reciprocal Teaching Model

The Reciprocal Teaching Model is an instructional approach in which the students become the teacher. This model provides instructional strategies that ultimately promote acceleration. This model can be introduced to any level of reader. However, it is best used for those students who can read fluently but may be showing difficulty in comprehension, as it is designed to enhance students' comprehension of a given text.

An additional benefit to using the reciprocal model is that it provides dialogue between students and the text and the teacher. This dialogue uses the four good-reader strategies: (1) *Predict*, (2) *Clarify*, (3) *Question*, and (4) *Summarize*.

Predicting

The predicting strategy requires students to use information and background knowledge to form a hypothesis about the author's intent. *By predicting, students acquire the ability to anticipate the information soon to be discovered in the text.* Once predictions are given, students realize that this sets the purpose for their reading experience. Prediction allows the student to link new knowledge learned to what they already know. Encourage students to check their predictions for accuracy once they have finished their reading experience.

Clarifying

The clarifying strategy encourages students to be aware of what they are reading in order for it to make sense. For various reasons, students often skip portions of what they read. *Self-correction of this omission by rereading text, looking for context clues, using pictures, or reading on does not always occur.* After introducing and using these strategies, teachers should encourage students to emphasize the strategies so that they can become habits.

Questioning

The most difficult of these four strategies may be the questioning strategy, since students having difficulty in comprehension usually do not stop to question the text. Questioning strategies and ideas can be found in Chapter 6 (pages 13 and 14).

The questioning strategy involves students in thinking about text before, during, and after reading. *Teachers should model using focus questions*—this is essential for students. Constant modeling and use of this strategy will enable students to recognize important information and organize it in the form of a higher-order question to self-test their understanding of the text.

Summarizing

Finally, the summarizing strategy encourages students to identify the most important information and to communicate it in a sequential manner. One may use the analogy of a *fist as the main idea* and the *fingers as the supporting details.* Without the two, the hand would not function well. Another analogy that lends itself to the understanding of a summary is the idea of the four walls in the classroom as details supporting the ceiling, which is the main idea. Students often confuse a summary for a retell. It is important that students recognize the difference so that they are confident in sorting through the information learned in their reading for (1) the *main idea* and (2) the *specific details that support it.*

The Reciprocal Teaching Model *(cont.)*

A typical reciprocal lesson is sequenced according to the following schedule.

Step One (5 Minutes)

Revisit previously read text.

Step Two (5 Minutes)

Review the previous day's reading, using a graphic organizer (the teacher or, as experience grows, preferably a student models the summarizing).

Step Three (5-10 Minutes)

Present a guided preview of new text, using specific vocabulary.

Step Four (10-15 Minutes)

Read and reciprocal teach. Remember that this entire process involves (1) predicting, (2) clarifying, (3) questioning, and (4) summarizing. In the process, the student ideally becomes a self-teacher.

Step Five (5 Minutes)

Respond and reflect (group organizer or questioning by students). If introduced early in the year, the reciprocal teaching model can be incorporated successfully in other discipline areas such as social studies and math problem solving.

Resources: E. Marie Mas, Director of Curriculum and Instruction, Easton, Redding and Regional 9 School Districts, Connecticut

Michelle Lindsay, Reading Specialist, Meriden Public Schools, Connecticut

The Question Answer Response (QAR) Model

The Strategy

What is the QAR Model? QAR is a reading strategy for students to use in order to organize comprehension questions according to where they got the information they needed to answer each question. Students are asked whether the information they used in their responses was textually *explicit*—that is, meaning it was "right there" in the text, or *implicit*—that is, meaning that they had to rely on the author and their own knowledge to find out what was being implied.

"Right there" answers are factual and based on what the author specifically tells the reader. Additional answers encouraged in the QAR model are *interpretive*—that is, ones that cause students to "think and search." Students put information together from different parts of the text to formulate a higher-order answer. "Author-and-me" responses encourage students to interpret what the author is saying while also relying on the students' own knowledge. Compare-and-contrast questions lend themselves to this level of response. Finally, students are encouraged to think on their own and provide a response that comes from the reader's own knowledge. *Critical stance* or *opinion* type questions support this level of QAR.

Combined with immediate feedback, QAR allows students to progress from shorter to longer texts and eventually to build independence from guided groups, leading to individual activities.

The Instructional Principles

QAR is based on four instructional principles:

1. Starting with factual questions (the answers to which are explicitly stated in the text) and progressing to questions based on longer text passages that require interpretive, applicative, or transactive level thinking (author-and-me questions)

2. Providing for supportive group instruction at the outset, followed by activities that require greater student independence

3. Providing immediate feedback to students

4. Moving from short text passages to longer, more involved text

In addition to knowing how to analyze the scoring rubric for their responses, students also need to know how to formulate teacher-like questions based on what they have read. If students are expected to respond to these types of questions on standardized tests, then they need to comprehend the questions and the task. Through constant modeling of good questioning techniques early in the year, students will gain confidence and independence in answering these higher-order questions.

The Question Answer Response (QAR) Model *(cont.)*

The Bookmark

In order to become successful in independent reading, reading groups, whole-group language groups, and this program, students themselves need to formulate questions before, during, and after they read. *A strong practice that will foster this skill is to provide your students with at least four focus-question bookmarks:* one for math problem-solving, one for the reading group folder, one for the independent reading folder, and one for any textbook to be used that day. By having the security of a bookmark that features key question stems, students feel competent in creating questions at their comfort level. Many students will stay with the "right there" questions at first, but over time they will begin to move beyond the text and initial understanding, learning to create and respond to higher-order questions.

The sample bookmark nearby illustrates how questions can be formulated and grouped according to four divisions:

- Right There Questions
- Think-and-Search Questions
- Author-and-Me Questions
- On-My-Own Questions

In each division the stems (or beginnings) of the questions prompt the students to learn to develop their own individual questions—to which, of course, they will write responses in their response notebooks.

A mini-lesson on introducing and using the QAR model can be found in Chapter 7 (page 28)

Adapted from *Teaching Children to Read and Write*, Robert R. Ruddell
Adapted from *Asking Better Questions*, The Wright Group

QAR Focus-Question Bookmark

Right There:

Who . . . ?

What . . . ?

Where . . . ?

When . . . ?

Think and Search:

What is meant by . . . ?

Can you describe . . . ?

What is the difference . . . ?

What is the main idea . . . ?

Author and Me:

Who would you choose . . . ?

What would happen if . . . ?

How would you . . . ?

Do you know someone like . . . ?

Why . . . ?

What if . . . ?

What was the purpose . . . ?

On My Own:

How could we/you . . . ?

Do you suppose that . . . ?

I wonder how . . . ?

Which is better . . . ?

Would you agree that . . . ?

Would it be better if . . . ?

What is your opinion . . . ?

Were they/you/we right to . . . ?

Chapter 7

Getting Started with Mini-Lessons

Before any students can self-select a text and then respond to it, they need modeling on how to do these things effectively. This modeling can be provided in mini-lessons that lend themselves to quick but strong instruction on the basic objective to be met.

Most language arts sessions can begin with a teacher-directed mini-lesson. Mini-lessons may be anywhere from 5 to 20 minutes long. The content of the lesson will often come from an analysis of what the students need to know next, combined with what the activity response on the calendar dictates. Specific mini-lessons may need to be repeated throughout the year to meet the needs of all students. After the instruction takes place, students will use the information from the mini-lesson immediately.

Sometimes the mini-lesson will be an introduction to a specific genre that is expected to be used immediately following the lesson. Sometimes the mini-lesson may encourage teacher and students to revisit a previously read text and analyze it in a new way—through the use of graphic organizers, shared writing, a teacher read-loud, readers theater, and other techniques. Again, the calendars will normally dictate the focus of the mini-lesson.

Mini-lessons can also focus on the different standardized testing strands and objectives. Mini-lessons offer the teacher the opportunity to show his or her own thinking and methods of attack when given a specific activity. Modeling is encouraged and should be used often. Demonstrate to students by thinking out loud, questioning, reading and writing, and creating higher-order questions as samples for their own question building.

Upon reflection, individual research, and reference to examples given in this book, teachers will be able to create their own specific mini-lessons of strong value for their classes. Such mini-lessons should support the calendars, lead to higher-order thinking, and develop effective student responses to their self-selected texts. The mini-lesson examples in this chapter focus on the following topics:

1. Self-Selection of Text (p. 16)
2. Elements of Fiction and Nonfiction (p. 17)
3. Responding to Text (p. 18)
4. Using Reciprocal Teaching Strategies (p. 21)
5. The QAR model (p. 28)
6. Analyzing and Understanding the Author's Craft (p. 29)
7. Analyzing and Understanding the Author's Purpose (p. 30)
8. Predicting What Will Happen (p. 33)
9. Choosing a Graphic Organizer (p. 34)

The order outlined above will benefit this independent reading program. Depending on schedules, curriculum, and testing periods, a teacher may present a mini-lesson a week, along with modeled instruction and guided practice for each focus. This regularity will benefit the students and the program. By taking the time early to present these training lessons, teachers will find that students will be more successful and independent as the year progresses. In addition, their responses will be of greater quality, having learned what is expected in a response.

Mini-Lesson 1:
Self-Selection of Text

Overview: Students must be able to think thoughtfully about the book they are selecting to read. Students must be able to choose a book that keeps their interest, to engage in the reading process, and to connect thoughtfully to what they are reading.

Objective: to analyze guidelines for self-selecting literature so that students will select a text appropriate for their ability and interest level

Resources/Materials: chart paper, markers, samples of text from all genres

Activities

1. Call students to the classroom library.

2. Display various examples of books from each genre.

3. Write the word *genre* on chart paper. Brainstorm ideas on what this word means. Chart the students' responses.

4. Discuss the word *genre* and define the word.

5. Following the discussion, chart different types of literature. Create a chart with brainstormed headings (*fiction, nonfiction, historical fiction, science fiction, history, mystery, science, reference,* etc.).

6. Review examples of books you have displayed and place each under the appropriate heading (picture book = fiction, dictionary = nonfiction/reference). Repeat with additional examples.

7. Review what it means to self-select any one of these books displayed. Organize self-selection guidelines into an ordered list (review of front cover, back cover, inside flap, summary of content, scan pages, author's name, examine the size of text, amount of text per page, number of pages).

8. Connect to the independent reading program the students will be participating in.

9. Review the importance of selecting books they are interested in.

10. Provide an opportunity for each student to select a book based on the guidelines charted.

Mini-Lesson 2: Elements of Fiction and Nonfiction

Overview: Students must be able to distinguish between a fiction and nonfiction text. By knowing the elements or aspects of each, they will be able to connect to the author's purpose and use each kind of text in order to meet their personal needs.

Objective: to analyze and recognize the elements of fiction and nonfiction in any given text

Resources/Materials: chart paper, markers, samples of text

Activities

1. Revisit the group-authored chart on genre. Discuss what the purpose of each genre might be.

2. Guide the students to think about what they know about fiction and nonfiction.

3. Display or draw a T-chart. Label it with headings of "Fiction" and "Nonfiction."

4. Divide students into cooperative groups of 4 to 5. Distribute stacks of fiction books to each group of students.

5. Allow students to preview and scan the texts in their groups.

6. Generate a list of elements found in fiction (*characters, setting, problem, solution, events, illustrations, make-believe*).

7. Chart all appropriate responses. Allow students to provide visual examples from the text by holding up the book when responding.

8. Repeat the activity using nonfiction books. Generate a list of elements and aspects found in books of nonfiction. Some guidance or prompting may be necessary (*headings, illustrations, subheadings, bolded words, cross-sections, maps, photographs, captions, graphs, charts, tables*).

9. Once all responses have been charted, review the group-authored T-chart. Check for understanding.

10. Provide each group with two books—one fiction and one nonfiction—and a Venn diagram. Instruct students to analyze the texts, compare and contrast what they find, and record it on the Venn diagram. Allow volunteers to share.

Mini-Lesson 3: Responding to Text

Overview: Students must be able to formulate complete sentences with an explanation connected to the text they have read. Students must be able to use evidence or details from the text to support the answers they have authored.

Objective: to form an understanding of and use the text to synthesize an answer to an open-ended question, using evidence from the text as support

Resources/Materials: various texts, response organizers, overhead projector

Activities

1. Instruct students that they will be expected to answer questions based on what they have read. Continue by explaining that they will be graded according to the scoring rubric (*see state mandated scoring rubric for open-ended responses or sample on page 68*).

2. Display the rubric on an overhead projector. Ask students to read the rubric silently.

3. Survey the class to see if any words need to be clarified (many hands will go up).

4. Take apart the rubric word by word, discussing each aspect and meaning. Turn each part into "kid-friendly" terms.

5. Given understanding of the rubric, display and/or distribute an open-ended question and answer. Allow the students to review the question, answer it, and then grade it according to the rubric. Instruct students that they are serving as the teacher in this action.

6. Allow students to read aloud their responses. Discuss their opinions. Remind students to use the rubric when explaining why they scored the question as they did.

7. Instruct students that they will be given the opportunity each day to respond to text and be graded according to this rubric.

8. The sample exercises on pages 19 and 20 will help students see different levels of response and how they may be evaluated by using the scoring rubric. These pages may be reproduced for distribution and/or projected overhead for discussion. (It is not necessary to read the original selection on which the exercise is based.)

Extension

Follow up this lesson with multiple opportunities to respond to text. Present a teacher read-aloud, modeling good reading behavior. After reading a teacher-selected text, allow students to respond to the text, reacting to the given focus of the lesson, such as *connection, visualizing, predicting, summarizing, critical stance/opinion,* or other strands and objectives aligned with the curriculum.

Mini-Lesson 3:
Responding to Text *(cont.)*

	Open-Ended Response Scoring Rubric
2	Response presents a reasonable explanation that answers the question. Response uses specific, relevant details from the passage as support.
1	Response presents a mostly reasonable explanation that answers the question. Response uses general information as support, rather than details from the passage.
0	Response presents an unreasonable explanation that does not answer the question. The response is vague.

Sample Exercise 1: (based on a passage from a book about the doomed ship *Titanic*)

Question:
Which information in the passage do you think is the most important? Use details from the passage to explain why you chose that information.

Answers:

1. There are many great features about the *Titanic* that make it safe. It has two bottoms. It has 16 watertight compartments in the lowest part of the *Titanic*. If a compartment starts to flood, the captain can pull a switch to close the door.

2. The *Titanic* is a large ship. It is four city blocks long and as tall as an 11-story building.

3. The *Titanic* cannot sink. It has two bottoms compared to other ships that have only one.

Which answer would receive a score of 2 and why?

Answer number _____ because _____

_____

_____

What specific details from the passage could be added to the other answers to improve scores?

_____

_____

Developed by Michelle Lindsay, Shelly Chordas, and Heidi Popielarczyk—Reading Specialists, Meriden Public Schools, Connecticut.

Mini-Lesson 3: Responding to Text *(cont.)*

	Open-Ended Response Scoring Rubric
2	Response presents a reasonable explanation that answers the question. Response uses specific, relevant details from the passage as support.
1	Response presents a mostly reasonable explanation that answers the question. Response uses general information as support, rather than details from the passage.
0	Response presents an unreasonable explanation that does not answer the question. The response is vague.

Sample Exercise 2: (based on a passage from a book about the doomed ship *Titanic*)

Question:
Using evidence from the passage, explain what a tour guide of the *Titanic* would say to visitors about the famous ship. Use specific details to support your answer.

The following response received a score of 1.

Please rewrite the response so it will receive a score of 2.

Welcome to the *Titanic*! The *Titanic* is a very large ship. It is believed to be unsinkable. There are many fancy rooms for you to visit. There is a grand staircase and a big dining room for you to eat in. The ship is considered to be very safe.

_____

_____

_____

_____

_____

_____

_____

_____

Developed by Michelle Lindsay, Shelly Chordas, and Heidi Popielarczyk—Reading Specialists, Meriden Public Schools, Connecticut.

Mini-Lesson 4: Using Reciprocal Teaching Strategies

Overview: The teacher will present a model of instruction involving four comprehension strategies that good readers must use before, during, and after they read.

Objective: to engage in the reading process, use the four basic comprehension strategies, and actively discuss their reading comprehension

Resources/Materials: various texts, response organizers, strategy cards, index cards

Activities

1. Write the word *reciprocal* on the board. Survey the class for the meaning or connection to the word.

2. Clarify the meaning of the word while informing students that they will be given the opportunity to be the teacher while reading.

3. Review what good readers do as they read. Guide the students to understand that as they read, good readers always do the following: (a) *predict*, (b) *clarify*, (c) *question*, and (d) *summarize*. Chart these four strategies.

4. Allow volunteers to share what they are reading independently. Allow students to share a strategy they most often use. Ask for an example of the strategy used.

5. Read aloud a favorite text, passage, or article that is an example of good literature. During the reading experience, model each of the four reading strategies.

6. Exchange roles and allow volunteers to predict, question, clarify, and summarize.

7. Instruct students that they will be responsible for using and modeling each of these strategies as they read with a group.

8. As a supplement to Mini-Lesson 4, see pages 22–27 for a reciprocal lesson-plan script and reciprocal lesson-plan template. Also, there are four follow-up lessons that use an instruct-prompt-survey pattern for the teacher to use in preparing students to understand each reciprocal strategy—predicting, clarifying, questioning, and summarizing.

Extension

Provide each student with four index cards. Instruct students to write each strategy on a card with sentence starters or prompts for each. Model how the cards can be used during group reading. Instruct students that as they read silently, they can hold the card up for the teacher to see what they are doing as they read at that particular time. Later, after reading silently in group, discuss how students used the strategy. Ask students to show in the text where they used that strategy.

Reciprocal Circle Reading Lesson Plan

Teacher Script

Date: _____ Time: _____

Group: _____

_____

- **Group Discussion of Independent Reading Books:** (Select two to three students.)

- **Strategy Reminder:** (What do you do when you predict? How can you help yourself if you get stuck reading? How does forming questions help you understand what you are reading? How do you summarize?) Students orally express how they will . . . .

- **Reading:** Shift to more silent reading, with some oral reading occasionally. Note strategy focus: predicting, questioning, clarifying, summarizing. (Example: Read pages _____ and develop two questions . . . .)

Pages:

_____

_____

_____

_____

- **Word Work:** List activity planned: making a words activity, listing words made from a larger word, vocabulary bingo or visualization, white-board writing, vocabulary categories, etc.

_____

_____

_____

- **Responding and Reflecting:** Students respond in any of the following ways—completing graphic organizers, reading a favorite part of the book, writing to a directed prompt response question, sharing orally a favorite part, writing three to six facts learned, using a double-entry journal, circle story, character traits charts, group mapping, etc. Circle the response activity completed.

- **Extended Activities:** research studies, biography studies, author studies

Developed by E. Marie Mas, Director Curriculum and Instruction, Easton, Redding and Regional 9 School Districts, Connecticut

Reciprocal Circle
Reading Lesson Plan *(cont.)*

Template

Date: _____   Time: _____

Group: _____

_____

- **Group Discussion of Independent Reading Books:** (Select two to three students.)

   List student names: _____

- **Strategy Reminder:** _____

- **Reading:** Note strategy focus: predicting, questioning, clarifying, summarizing

Pages:

_____

_____

_____

_____

- **Word Work:**

_____

_____

_____

_____

- **Responding and Reflecting:** Students respond in any of the following ways—completing graphic organizers, reading a favorite part of the book, writing to a directed prompt response question, sharing orally a favorite part, writing three to six facts learned, using a double-entry journal, circle story, character traits charts, group mapping, etc. Circle the response activity completed.

- **Graphic Organizer Selected** _____

- **Extended Activities:** _____

   Developed by E. Marie Mas, Director Curriculum and Instruction, Easton, Redding and Regional 9 School Districts, Connecticut

Reciprocal Strategy: Predicting

1. **Instruct students:** Good readers predict as they read. When reading a fiction story, we can predict what we think will happen next in the story by looking at the *text clues*. These clues can be found in *chapter titles, pictures,* and *what we have already read.* When reading a nonfiction book, we can predict what we will learn next by using text clues like *chapter headings, pictures, captions, photographs, maps,* and *diagrams.*

2. **During reading or after reading in class, use the following prompts with students:**

Fiction

- Based on the title, what do you think this story/chapter will be about?
- What do you already know about _____?
- What do you think will happen in this chapter?
- How do you think the problem will be resolved?
- What do you think the main character will do next?

Nonfiction

- Based on the title, what do you think this book/chapter will be about?
- What do you already know about the topic?
- What do you think you will learn?
- What would happen if _____?
- Why do you think the author wrote about this topic?

3. **Survey students:** How does using the "predict" strategy help us as we read?

_____

_____

_____

_____

_____

_____

_____

_____

Adapted from Raquel Forte, Fifth Grade Teacher, Connecticut

Reciprocal Strategy: Clarifying

1. **Instruct students:** Good readers clarify as they read. They clarify when the text they are reading may be hard to understand. Readers should clarify when . . .

   A. They do not know how to SAY A WORD.

   B. They do not understand the WORD IS MEANING.

   C. They do not know what an ENTIRE SENTENCE or GROUP OF WORDS means.

2. **During reading or after reading in class, use the following prompts with students:**

   • What did the author mean when he/she wrote _____?

   • Who can clarify the word meaning for _____?

   • What do you know about the word _____?

   • What did the author mean by the word _____?

   • What does the author mean by the whole sentence_____?

   • What does the author mean by the phrase _____?

   • What is the author trying to say by the phrase _____?

   • Choose one word or phrase you do not understand. _____

   • Create one question you would like answered by the author. _____

   • What is one question you still have about _____?

3. **Survey students:** How does using the "clarify" strategy help us as we read?

   _____

   _____

   _____

   _____

   _____

   _____

   Adapted from Raquel Forte, Fifth Grade Teacher, Connecticut

Reciprocal Strategy: Questioning

1. **Instruct students:** Good readers question before, during, and after they read. Asking questions helps you to understand what you are reading.

2. **During reading or after reading in class, use the following prompts with students** (*you may also use the focus-question bookmark*):

   - How does the author compare _____ and _____?

   - What questions would you ask the author/character/object ? _____

   - What questions do you have about _____?

   - What do you want to learn about _____?

   - Can you connect this reading experience to self/book/friend/world ? _____

   - What questions would you like to ask the author ? _____

   - What was the purpose of _____?

   - Which would be better . . . _____

     or _____?

3. **Survey students:** How does using the "question" strategy help us as we read?

   _____

   _____

   _____

   _____

   _____

   _____

   _____

   _____

   _____

   _____

   _____

Adapted from Raquel Forte, Fifth Grade Teacher, Connecticut

Reciprocal Strategy: Summarizing

1. **Instruct students:** Good readers summarize main events and ideas as they read. When we summarize, we tell in our own words about what we have read.

2. **During reading or after reading in class, use the following prompts with students** (*be sure they summarize without looking at the text*):

   Fiction

   - What is this story mainly about? _____

   - Who are the main characters in this story? _____

   - What is/are the problem(s) in this story? _____

   - How was/were the problem(s) resolved? _____

   Nonfiction

   - What did you learn about_____?

   - If someone asked you about _____what would you tell them?

   - What facts did you find interesting in this section/chapter?

   - How are _____and _____ alike?

   - How are _____and _____ different?

   - What is this paragraph/section mostly about? _____

   - What is the main idea of this paragraph/section? _____

3. **Survey students:** How does using the "summarize" strategy help us as we read?

   _____

   _____

   _____

   _____

   _____

   _____

   _____

Adapted from Raquel Forte, Fifth Grade Teacher, Connecticut

Mini-Lesson 5: The QAR Model

Overview: Students must be able to question the text before, during, and after they have read in order to increase comprehension.

Objective: for students to recognize and use focus question stems in the QAR model when reading and discussing a text

Resources/Materials: pre-programmed chart of QAR strategy (bulletin board), chart paper, reading passages or sample texts, QAR bookmark, overhead projector

Activities

1. Display chart or use an interactive bulletin board of the QAR model. Instruct students that it is time to start asking better questions when reading a given text.

2. Distribute copies of the focus-question QAR Bookmark (see Chapter 10: Reproducibles, page 71). Review the questions of each level. Remind students that the question stems they see are all good. Encourage students to move up and down or in and out of each level of questioning.

3. Display a short reading passage overhead. Instruct students to read silently while you read aloud. Instruct students that when they have finished reading they are to use their bookmark as a guide to form a teacher-like question that can be answered from the text.

4. Model a good teacher-like question that can be answered from the text. Discuss the level of question and how it helps the reader to understand what has been read.

5. Allow students to share their questions. Allow each student to be the teacher and call on another to answer it. They may grade the answers according to the scoring rubric.

6. Repeat and reinforce the use of the bookmark each day.

Extensions: Read aloud passages from social studies, science, an anthology, and weekly periodicals, encouraging students to formulate questions with the bookmark.

Use the bookmark as a review for a quiz. Students can create three focus questions to ask their classmates.

Mini-Lesson 6: Analyzing and Understanding the Author's Craft

Overview: Students must be able to analyze the art of writing—techniques that help the reader connect with the text through the author's love of writing, passion for literature, and skill at using language to create clear images in the reader's mind.

Objective: for the students to analyze the author's craft in order to comprehend what has been read, to connect the text to personal/outside experiences, and to analyze various literary devices used by the author

Resources/Materials: various activities on literary devices, various text using a specific literary device, chart paper, markers, blank paper

Activities

1. Survey students as to why they think people write books. Chart responses.

2. Discuss that authors generally have a love of writing for their audience (readers). They also like to "play" with words in such a way as to paint a picture in the reader's mind.

3. Distribute a sheet of blank paper. Instruct students to fold it in half vertically to create a T-chart. Model how to fold and label it.

4. Instruct students to label one side of the chart with the heading of "Key Words and Phrases" and the other with "Produces Strong Images about . . ."

5. Instruct students to record any key words or phrases they hear as a poem is read aloud. Allow students to record the title of the poem at the top of the chart.

6. Read a poem aloud.

7. Upon reading, allow time for students to think about the images these words produced in their minds.

8. Allow volunteers to share the images.

9. Choose specific teaching moments to discuss a given literary device used by the author. Point out that this device is one part of the craft or art of writing.

10. Allow students to draw a picture to connect to the image they saw in their mind.

11. Students can reflect on what these words tell them about the craft of writing and how they can use what they have learned.

Extensions: Generate a list of literary devices used by authors to deepen the interpretation of the text. Chart responses and keep them visible in the classroom.

Provide weekly investigations on various devices encouraging students to review, interpret, and use the device in many disciplines. Some examples of these are as follows:

- Similes
- Metaphors
- Powerful verbs
- Alliteration
- Analogies
- Portmanteau words
- Hyperboles

Mini-Lesson 7: Analyzing and Understanding the Author's Purpose

Overview: Students must be able to figure out why an author wrote a particular text. Students should question the text and find reasons why the piece was written.

Objective: for students to analyze the text for reasons the author wrote the text (purpose)

Resources/Materials: chart paper, various texts, Activity A and Activity B (pages 31 and 32)

Activities

1. Survey the students as to why they think authors write what they write. Guide the students to realize that authors write to inform or teach—that is, to *entertain* or *persuade* or *convince* their readers.

2. Discuss the meaning of each of the above. Display and read aloud an example of each. Survey whether students agree that the specific text is an example of that purpose.

3. Distribute Activity A (page 31) of mini passages. Model problems 1 and 2. Read aloud while modeling and think aloud of how to analyze the text in order to comprehend the author's purpose.

4. After students have developed understanding/mastery, allow them to complete activity pages A and B. Allow volunteers to share. Discuss each problem to check for understanding.

5. Instruct students that they will need to analyze the texts they read daily to explain what the purpose of each was.

   Extension: Follow up with a teacher read-aloud and CLOZE passages throughout the week.

   (*Cloze passages are reading selections from which elements have been systematically deleted, leaving blank spaces for the reader to fill with logically appropriate terms.*)

Analyzing and Understanding the Author's Purpose

Activity A   Name _____

Directions: Determine the author's purpose for each passage. Decide whether the passage is to inform, persuade, or entertain the reader.

1. When the space shuttle reaches outer space, it is beyond the pull of gravity. The lack of gravity, the force that pulls objects toward Earth, results in weightlessness. For most astronauts, the experience of being weightless is interesting and enjoyable.

   What is the author's purpose for writing this passage?

   _____

   _____

2. Amy was riding her bicycle home from school when suddenly a squirrel jumped in front of her and stood on his hind legs. She squeezed the brakes on her handle bars so hard that she almost fell over them. Amy looked at the squirrel, puzzled. It was as though the squirrel wanted to tell her something. The squirrel cocked his head, spit an acorn out of his mouth, and ran away.

   What is the author's purpose for writing this passage?

   _____

   _____

3. Ralph Rotten's tasty Apple Ripple Dipple ice cream is the greatest thing on this side of town. If your mouth does not water after your first bite, we'll refund your money. This special blend of apples, caramel, and cream will make all your worries disappear. Visit Ralph Rotten's today and receive a free cone to hold your scoops.

   What is the author's purpose for writing this passage?

   _____

   _____

Adapted from Linda Owns, 2001

Analyzing and Understanding The Author's Purpose

Activity B   Name _____

Directions: Determine the author's purpose for each passage. Decide whether the passage is to inform, persuade, or entertain the reader. Explain in writing why you think the way you do, using evidence from the passage to support your answer.

1. Speedy computers are very user friendly. We can deliver them right to your door in 24 hours. Act fast. These computers are selling out quickly. Don't be the only one in your neighborhood without this state-of-the-art Speedy computer. The cost for this special package is $399.00. This offer will only last for two more days. Send your check now to P.O. Box 1234, South Berry, Maine 55000.

   What is the author's purpose for writing this passage? _____

   _____

   Why do you think the way you do? _____

   _____

2. A portmanteau word is usually a noun. It is a word created by combining or blending two words into one. An example of a portmanteau word is "brunch," which can be made from breakfast and lunch. Another example is "squiggle," which can be made from squirm and wiggle.

   What is the author's purpose for writing this passage? _____

   _____

   Why do you think the way you do? _____

   _____

3. My brother once blew a bubble so big, that when it popped it spattered all over his face. It got stuck in his hair, nose, and eyelashes. Mom had to use peanut butter to get it out of his hair. You should have seen the peanut butter on his eyelashes.

   What is the author's purpose for writing this passage? _____

   _____

   Why do you think the way you do? _____

   _____

Adapted from Linda Owns, 2001

Mini-Lesson 8: Predicting What Will Happen

Overview: Students must be able to move beyond the text and predict what will happen based on what they have read. Students must be able to evaluate the text.

Objective: for students to predict and anticipate what will happen next in the text and use evidence to support the prediction

Resources/Materials: literature samples or CLOZE passages, prediction organizer (see Chapter 10: Reproducibles, page 75) and copies for each student, overhead projector

Activities

1. Review the good reader strategies used within the reciprocal model (see page 11).

2. Instruct students that they will use what they have read to make a prediction of what will happen next. Then they will locate evidence from the text that supports their prediction and evidence contrary to their prediction.

3. Display the prediction organizer overhead. Review headings and guidelines for completing the chart. Distribute a chart to each student. You may want students to draw the chart to help them practice creating a chart that organizes their writing and information.

4. Display an appropriate CLOZE passage or reading sample. Display one paragraph at a time, so students can predict what will happen or be learned in the next paragraph. Read the text aloud while students read silently. Model thinking aloud and the use of clarifying and questioning strategies.

5. After reading one paragraph, instruct students to record in the first column what they believe will happen next. Encourage students to write a complete response by using "I'll bet . . . ," "I think . . . ," "I predict . . . ," "I infer . . . ," or "I guess . . . ."

6. Instruct students to record textual details that support their prediction in the second column and textual evidence that does not support their prediction in the third column.

7. Display and read aloud the next paragraph. Allow students to check their predictions for accuracy.

8. Repeat step five until the passage is read in its entirety.

9. Survey the class for a summary of what has been learned by completing this activity. Reinforce the importance of using text support when predicting. Remind students that predicting and anticipating what will happen in a text will prepare them and help them build a stronger understanding of what has been read.

Resources: Connecticut Mastery Test Third Generation Language Arts Handbook

Mini-Lesson 9: Choosing a Graphic Organizer

Overview: Students must be able to focus on information in the text and then choose a specific type of organizer based on purpose, text characteristics, and personal preference.

Objective: for students to analyze the text and practice organizational strategies by choosing an appropriate graphic organizer to arrange, organize, summarize, sequence, or compare the text

Resources/Materials: graphic organizers to display (see pages 35–36), selected reading passage to display and distribute, overhead projector, blank paper

Activity

1. Write the words *graphic organizer* on the board or overhead. Survey the students to see if they know what this means. Discuss the meanings of the words *graphic* (picture, relating to the visual arts, diagram, vividly realistic) and *organizer* (give orderly structure, arrange).

2. Following students' understanding of the term, display overhead samples of organizers (see pages 35–36) Review the purpose of each organizer.

3. Instruct students that they will practice choosing an organizer to display or arrange information learned from the text. Display and distribute the reading passage you have selected. Formulate a question for students to answer using a graphic organizer of their choice:

   a. Which graphic organizer would you choose to compare and contrast X and Y?

   b. Which graphic organizer would you choose to sequence the events in order?

   c. Which graphic organizer would you choose to summarize what you have read?

   d. Which graphic organizer would you choose to show how the actions of the main character/person had an effect on others?

   e. Which graphic organizer would you choose to show how the problem was solved?

   f. Which graphic organizer would you choose to show your background knowledge and questions for what you want to learn as you read?

   Provide each student with blank paper to draw and complete the appropriate organizer with information from the text.

4. Provide additional questions so students can draw and complete additional organizers.

5. Instruct students that they will be responsible for choosing the shape of an organizer based on the purpose of the text and the information learned. Remind students that using various types of organizers helps them to practice different types of organizational strategies, especially in note-taking.

Resources: Michelle Lindsay, Reading Specialist, Meriden Public Schools, Connecticut

Which Graphic Organizer Would You Choose?

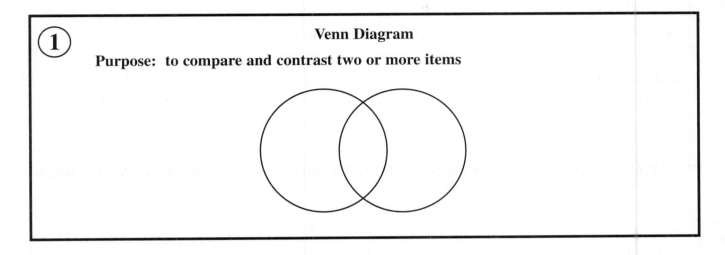

① **Venn Diagram**

Purpose: to compare and contrast two or more items

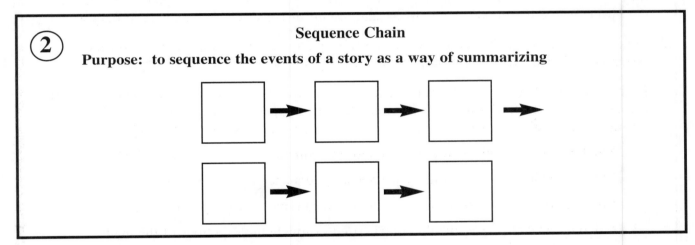

② **Sequence Chain**

Purpose: to sequence the events of a story as a way of summarizing

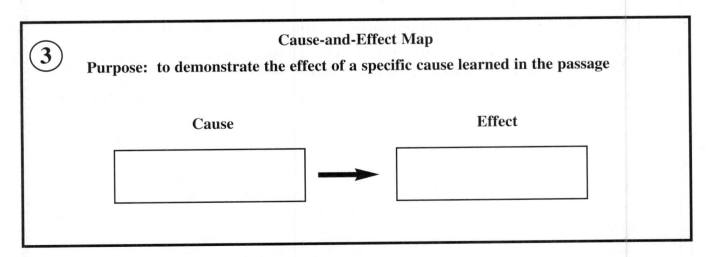

③ **Cause-and-Effect Map**

Purpose: to demonstrate the effect of a specific cause learned in the passage

Cause   Effect

Which Graphic Organizer Would You Choose? *(cont.)*

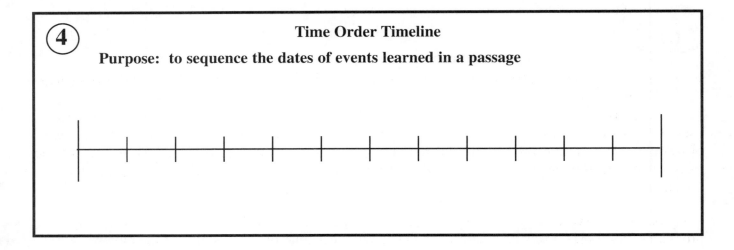

④ **Time Order Timeline**

Purpose: to sequence the dates of events learned in a passage

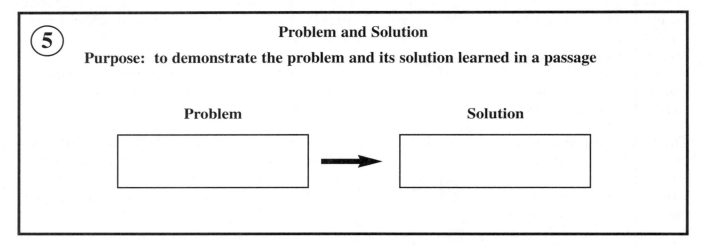

⑤ **Problem and Solution**

Purpose: to demonstrate the problem and its solution learned in a passage

Problem   Solution

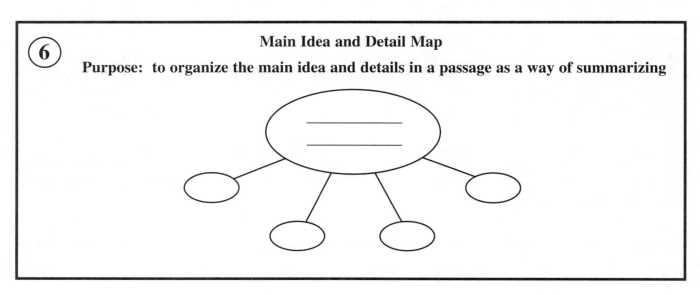

⑥ **Main Idea and Detail Map**

Purpose: to organize the main idea and details in a passage as a way of summarizing

Open-Ended Response Calendars

Creating a response calendar is easy. Choosing what the response should be can be difficult. There is so much research and literature on how to formulate questions to foster higher-order thinking that it can be hard to choose a response. One may use many resources to help formulate the response questions. Reading departments and reading teams often create tools that can be used in the classroom to create higher-order questions.

A great resource in formulating higher-order questions is a bookmark prepared by Dr. Sue Deffenbaugh (see Chapter 10: Reproducibles, pages 72 and 73). Aligned with standardized testing strands and objectives, this tool is a good aid in the preparation of related bookmarks that are tailored for specific uses and types of reading in the classroom. These related bookmarks then lend themselves to all areas of learning. As mentioned in the introduction, it is wise to seek out information on the QAR model, the Reciprocal Teaching model, state standardized testing strands and objectives, and, of course, Bloom's Taxonomy.

The reading response calendar is definitely the most important tool within an independent reading program of this type. You should introduce the monthly calendar on the first day of the month. Distribute a copy to each student. Students should keep the calendar in the response folders. Introduce the response activity each day in order to clarify the expectations or use their response as a mini-lesson for instruction on a specific focus for the day. At this point, it is helpful to incorporate standardized testing strands and objectives. It can be challenging to meet these objectives each day. As teachers know, there is just not enough time. However, by using these 15- to 20-minute responses that spiral from month to month through the use of authentic text, teachers and students will be meeting standardized testing objectives daily.

The reading response calendars included in this book (pages 38–63) are generic. This means that they can be applied to any classroom, anywhere. (Teachers will, however, want to scan these calendars to see if certain topics are not yet within their classroom library.) Specific dates can be inserted for the month in any given year. A blank 25-day calendar is also included if the programmed calendars do not meet the needs of your classroom or if you wish to amend any of the ones presented in this book.

Ultimately, the monthly calendars supplied here will serve as a springboard for you to start your independent reading program. As time and experience dictate, you will develop additional questions, prompts, and responses to enrich your program. There are many calendar creator programs available. Information and response questions can be easily inserted, as well as clip art to add visual appeal for computers. You will want to experiment with these, but it is wise to remain focused on the effective response questions that are being provided for the students. Display a copy of the monthly calendar in the area that has been designated as the independent reading response section within the classroom library.

Finally, knowing that 25 days of quality lessons or response activities are in place for the month will lead to a secure feeling for any teacher charged with managing an independent reading program. One less thing to worry about!

September

Monday	Tuesday	Wednesday	Thursday	Friday
Revisit a text you read this summer. Connect to a personal summer experience and plan a picnic to celebrate reading. Make a list telling whom you would invite and what you would eat.	Select a book on nutrition. Brainstorm a list of things to eat for breakfast. Draw a picture of your favorite breakfast. Write the recipe in sequence so a friend can make it too!	Revisit your text from Monday. Plan a final trip you would like to take this summer. Write a story telling with descriptive words where you would go and what you would do.	In your journal, design a special hat you would choose to wear on your trip. Explain your design using descriptive words.	**Visit the Library!** Choose a book to read in an unusual place. Describe your reading experience. Retell your favorite part of the book and explain why it is your favorite.
Visit the Library! Select a fairy tale book. Choose the part of the story that you think was MOST important and explain why you think the way you do.	Revisit the fairy tale you selected and read. Recall which character you would most like to be. Give at least five reasons why you think the way you do.	Revisit your fairy tale. Using the text and pictures, make a map about the setting of your book. Add color and labels so that a friend can follow your map.	Choose a graphic organizer to compare and contrast the neighborhood you live in and the neighborhood or setting described in your fairy tale. Draw and complete the organizer.	Choose a main character from your fairy tale. Create five interview questions you could ask. Create answers to the questions that could be answered by the main character.
Visit the Library! Select a book about insects. Choose an insect to investigate. Write down five facts you learned about your insect and draw a picture next to each fact.	Revisit your insect book. Write down five questions you would like to ask an insect expert.	**Visit the Library!** Select a book that interests you. Look for similes. A simile is a comparison using "like" or "as." Choose a simile from the story and explain why the author used it.	Revisit a favorite book you have read. What did you think about while you were reading the text? Give evidence from the text or personal experiences to support your answer.	**Visit the Library!** Select a fiction book of your choice. What is the problem in the story? Give specific details from the text to support your answer.

Open-Ended Response Calendars

September *(cont.)*

Monday	Tuesday	Wednesday	Thurdsday	Friday
Visit the Library! Select a book by a favorite or known author. Pretend you are the author and describe the part of the book that was most fun to write and explain why.	Think about the author you chose. Write a letter to the author and explain your reaction to the book. Use details from the text to support your first reaction.	Recall your reading and writing experience from yesterday. If you were an alien from Mars, how would you react to this book? Would your reaction be similar or different? Tell why.	**Visit the Library!** Choose a book to read. Make a bookmark showing the best part of the book. Explain why you think this way.	Revisit a fiction book or choose a new one to read. Based on the information in the story, in the future what will MOST LIKELY happen? Use information from the text to support your answer.
Visit the Library! Select a fiction book of your choice. Choose a word to clarify. Use context clues and complete this sentence. "You can tell from what is said in the story that ____ means . . ."	Revisit your fiction book. Pretend you are one of the characters and write a diary or journal entry about what happened to you in today's reading.	Write a paragraph about a book you have read, explaining why you think it could or could not be made into a movie. If you make it into a movie, list who would star in it and what the title might be.	Recall the books you have read this summer and write a letter to your teacher that tells about all of the great books you have read.	Revisit any book you have read this month. Scan the text and briefly summarize the story. Use evidence from the text to support your summary.
		Notes		

October

Monday	Tuesday	Wednesday	Thursday	Friday
Visit the Library! Select a picture book to read. Write down what the lesson or theme is of the story.	Revisit the picture book you chose. Fill a page in your journal writing about the main character, beginning with the sentence: "I was ___ (any verb) by . . . ."	Reflect on your reading experiences so far. Write five reasons why reading is good for you.	**Visit the Library!** Choose a book about friends. Write about what the friends do together. Provide examples to support your answers.	Connect to your reading experience. Draw a picture of a special friend. Write a poem about your special friend.
Visit the Library! Select a nonfiction book of your choice. Record all of the aspects of nonfiction you found in your book	Revisit a nonfiction book of your choice. Review the aspects and elements of nonfiction. Choose one and explain why it is important to the text.	**Visit the Library!** Select a nonfiction book connecting to a topic in class. Review the headings in the book and rewrite them in your journal. Are these helpful to you? Why?	**Visit the Library!** Select a fiction and nonfiction book. Choose a graphic organizer to compare and contrast the characteristics of each genre. Draw and complete the organizer.	Review your journal entry from Wednesday. Choose five headings and rewrite them as questions that can be answered from the text.
Visit the Library! Select a book about an animal. Choose an animal to investigate. Write down five facts you learned about your animal and draw a picture next to each fact.	Revisit your animal book. Write down five questions you would like to ask an animal expert.	**Visit the Library!** Select a book that you can read with a partner. Create a ten-question quiz that can be answered by reading the story.	Revisit a favorite book you have read. Make connections to yourself, another book you have read, and to the world around you.	**Visit the Library!** Select a fiction book. Write and complete this sentence: "The character can BEST be described as ___." Give specific details for support.

October (cont.)

Monday	Tuesday	Wednesday	Thurdsday	Friday
Visit the Library! Select and read a nonfiction book. Write a commercial telling why someone should read this book. Draw pictures if needed.	Revisit any book you have read. Draw and complete a four-panel (boxes) comic strip showing four events that happened in your book. Write a sentence about each picture.	**Visit the Library!** Share a book with four friends. Discuss all the story elements you find. Write a summary of your reading experience with your "book club."	**Visit the Library!** Choose a book about Halloween. Invent a new candy bar to sell. Describe the ingredients and draw a picture of this new candy bar.	Revisit a fiction book or choose a new book to read. Explain how the main character solved his or her problem. Give specific information from the story to support your answer.
Visit the Library! Select a dictionary or other reference book. Review how it is organized. List what you noticed about the structure of the text. Is this structure helpful?	Look through a dictionary. Find and write the meaning of the word *genius*. Would you like to be a genius? Explain why or why not.	Sketch a poster that advertises a dictionary. Below the sketch, write five to seven sentences that describe a dictionary. Try to persuade a classmate to love the dictionary.	Revisit any books read about Halloween or the season. Create an acrostic poem using a word from the text. Use details from the text to complete your poem.	Revisit any book you have read this month. Scan the text and briefly tell how two characters are alike or different. Be sure to give specific information to support your answer.

Notes

November

Monday	Tuesday	Wednesday	Thursday	Friday
Visit the Library! Select a book about a topic you are learning. List eight vocabulary words from the book. Using context clues, write each definition and page number where it can be found.	Choose a word from your vocabulary list. Make an illustration showing what it looks like. Write a meaning-loaded sentence beneath your picture and a sentence from the text where the word can be found.	Read and write five interesting facts about your topic. Draw a picture next to each fact. Be sure to use your text from Monday to support your answers.	Revisit your facts. Now revisit the text and find five opinions the author mentioned in the text.	Switch journals with a partner. Read the entries of this week and comment on each. State whether you learned something new or agree with the entries. Be supportive and constructive in your responses.
Visit the Library! Select a favorite book to read. Write and complete this sentence: "If the author added another paragraph to the end of the story, it would MOST likely describe . . . ."	Find an exciting picture or illustration in any book or magazine. Write a story telling what might have been happening.	**Visit the Library!** Select a book to read. Explain why you chose this book. After reading the text, explain if you would or would not recommend this book to a friend.	Recall any book you have read. Imagine you are one of the characters. Write a journal or diary entry about what happened to you.	**Visit the Library!** Select a fiction book of your choice. Write a different ending to the story. Defend your ending by stating why you think the story should end this way.
Visit the Library! Select a book about early settlers or pilgrims. Write down five facts you learned about the settlers or pilgrims and draw a picture next to each fact.	Revisit your early settler or pilgrim book and facts learned. Imagine you were giving a speech about this topic. What would you say in your speech? Use details to support your answer.	Imagine that you are spending the night in a pilgrim or colonial village. Describe what you think your first night of sleep might be like. Use details to enhance your story.	Revisit your nonfiction text from Monday. Why do you think the author emphasizes the hardships of early settlers/pilgrims or colonists?	Reflect on your reading experience this week. Connect the reading to yourself, another text, and to your world.

November *(cont.)*

Monday	Tuesday	Wednesday	Thurdsday	Friday
Visit the Library! Select a fiction book to read. Write a paragraph explaining the appearance or personality of the character. Include page numbers where the information can be found.	Revisit the book you chose on Monday. Choose a graphic organizer to sequence the events as they took place in the story. Draw and complete the organizer.	Reflect on your Tuesday entry. Write a summary of what you think of the events that took place in the story you selected.	Switch journals with a partner. Respond to five entries. Tell your partner what you liked or agreed with.	**Visit the Library!** Choose a book to read. Make a bookmark showing the best part of the book. Explain why you think this way.
Visit the Library! Select a biography. Review the aspects of nonfiction. Do you agree with how the author organized the text? Explain.	Select a fiction book you have read. Compare this text to the biography you chose. List the similarities and differences you find.	Draw a picture of the person in your biography. Write a two-sentence caption about the illustration.	Choose a word from your biography to clarify. Use any resource to locate its meaning and write a sentence using the word and its meaning.	Revisit any book you have read this month. Scan the text and briefly summarize the story.
		Notes		

December

Monday	Tuesday	Wednesday	Thursday	Friday
Visit the Library! Select a poem to read. Draw a picture of what the poem makes you think of. Write the title and the author of the poem.	**Visit the Library!** Select a nonfiction book to read. Write the proper nouns you find in your book. Draw a picture for five of the proper nouns you located.	**Visit the Library!** Select a book about a historical person. Write at least five important things he or she did.	Reflect on your reading experience yesterday. Rewrite and complete this sentence: "You can tell from this text that the author thinks . . . ."	Using the historical facts read this week, write a poem about the historical person. Your poem does not have to rhyme.
Visit the Library! Select a nonfiction book of your choice. Imagine you are writing a letter to the author. What two questions not already answered in the text would you ask?	Revisit a nonfiction book of your choice. Rewrite and complete this sentence: "You can tell from the information in the text that . . . ."	**Visit the Library!** Select a book about winter. Draw a picture and write two sentences to describe what you have read.	**Visit the Library!** Select a book about winter or snow. Connect to the text and write about a time you played in the snow.	Revisit the text chosen on Wednesday. Review the organization of the text. Did the author's structure of the text help you to understand the features of winter? Explain.
Visit the Library! Select a fiction book of your choice. Quote at least five passages of good description and good dialogue and explain the purpose of each.	Revisit a familiar book of your choice. Make a list of ten words from the text. Use a thesaurus to locate and write synonyms of each word.	**Visit the Library!** Select a book that you can read with a partner. Discuss and write in your journal why the book begins the way it does.	**Visit the Library!** Select a book of your choice. Write down the author's purpose (reason) for writing this book. Use details to support your thoughts and opinions.	Use a dictionary to look up the word *resolution.* Write the definition and five resolutions you have for yourself in the new year.

December *(cont.)*

Monday	Tuesday	Wednesday	Thurdsday	Friday
Visit the Library! Select and read a nonfiction book about any state. Write down five facts about the state and the page numbers to prove your details.	Using the facts learned Monday about a state, write a brief summary highlighting the important facts about your state.	Choose a graphic organizer to compare and contrast another state with the state you have been researching. Draw and complete the graphic organizer.	**Visit the Library!** Choose a book about holidays. How can you tell that the author cares about the topic he or she is writing about? Use details to support your opinion.	Write about your winter vacation and what you plan to do with your family. Share your plans and a favorite book with a friend.
Visit the Library! Select a fiction book. Write about the job or career the main character has. What did you learn about the job?	Revisit your fiction book from Monday. Create a job application for the main character in the book. Fill in each part of the application.	Sketch a poster of your main character. Write a caption under your illustration that makes him or her Employee of the Month.	**Visit the Library!** Revisit or choose any book about winter or snow. Connect by imagining you find a magical snowmobile. Write about the adventure you have with this snowmobile.	Illustrate one scene from your magical snowmobile adventure, using a pencil sketch or color.
		Notes		

January

Monday	Tuesday	Wednesday	Thursday	Friday
Visit the Library! Select a nonfiction book. Turn to the tenth page in your book. Write the main idea and four supporting details	Revisit your nonfiction text from Monday. What question does the second paragraph answer? Explain how the author was able to answer this question.	**Visit the Library!** Select a familiar text. Locate a word to teach a classmate. Rewrite and complete this sentence: "In this text, the word _____ means . . . ."	Using your text from Wednesday, draw and complete a sequence chain highlighting the important events in the text.	Review your journal entries. Checkmark the entries that you are proud of. Write a reflection of why they are important to you.
Visit the Library! Select an encyclopedia. Open it to a page anywhere in the text. Write down five facts learned on this page.	Revisit the page selected on Monday. Continue researching this topic and write five new facts learned. Draw a picture to illustrate the MOST interesting fact learned.	Share your research topic and facts learned with a partner. Respond to the information in each other's journal. Be sure to give an opinion of the information learned.	Choose a graphic organizer to compare and contrast your research topic to something or someone in your world. Draw and complete the organizer.	Using information learned this week, write any kind of poem about your topic. Your poem does not have to rhyme.
Reflect on and record what you already know about Martin Luther King, Jr. List at least five things you know.	**Visit the Library!** Select a book about Martin Luther King, Jr. What is your opinion of this man and his actions?	Revisit your book on Martin Luther King, Jr. Write down five facts that can be learned from your text.	Using your book choice from Tuesday, rewrite and complete this sentence: "In this story, the word *dream* means . . . ."	Reflect on your reading experience this week. List five reasons why it is important to have a hope or dream for something or someone.

January *(cont.)*

Monday	Tuesday	Wednesday	Thurdsday	Friday
Visit the Library! Do you have a dream or hope for the world? Write about what it is.	Revisit or select any text on Martin Luther King, Jr. Reflect and write one thing you would change for the future. Share your ideas with a partner.	**Visit the Library!** Select a fiction book. Read and think of a situation in the story. Write down how you would have handled it differently.	**Visit the Library!** Choose a book to read. Write a song about the main character, sung to a tune like "Row, Row, Row Your Boat" or "Twinkle, Twinkle, Little Star	Revisit a fiction book or choose a new one to read. Based on the story, what will most likely happen next? Use information from the text to support your answer.
Visit the Library! Select a book from any genre. Rewrite and complete this sentence: "The main idea of this text is . . . "	Revisit your book choice from Monday. Write a letter in your journal to a friend, telling him or her your thoughts about the reading.	**Visit the Library!** Select a book you have never read. Write a paragraph explaining how you would change the story if you could.	**Visit the Library!** Select a book connecting to a topic in class. Write down ten interesting words from the text. Write them in new creative sentences.	Revisit any book you have read this month. Scan the text and briefly summarize the story.
		Notes		

February

Monday	Tuesday	Wednesday	Thursday	Friday
Visit the Library! Select a nonfiction book. List ten words to clarify. Solve your problem and write what resources you used to clarify each.	Use a dictionary to help you understand the words located on Monday. Choose two words to illustrate and rewrite in meaning-loaded sentences.	**Visit the Library!** Select a book of your choice. Create ten teacher-like questions that can be answered from the text.	**Visit the Library!** Choose a book about an interesting topic. Read and choose the parts of the reading that you think are MOST important.	Reflect on your reading experiences and write a letter to your teacher explaining your favorite and least favorite thing about reading.
Visit the Library! Select a book about a famous African American. Write five interesting contributions this person made to the world. Draw a picture next to your favorite fact.	Revisit a nonfiction book of your choice. Review the aspects of nonfiction found. Choose one and explain why it is important to the text.	**Visit the Library!** Select a nonfiction book connecting to a topic in class. Review the graphics in the text. Record what you found and whether or not these graphics are helpful to you. Explain why or why not.	**Visit the Library!** Select a nonfiction book. Choose a graphic organizer to compare and contrast two aspects of nonfiction in your text. Draw and complete the organizer.	Review your journal entry from Wednesday. Choose two graphics and create teacher-like questions that can be answered by interpreting the graphic.
Visit the Library! Select a fiction book. Rewrite and complete this sentence: "This (character/person) reminds me of . . ."	Revisit your fiction book from Monday. Create a T-chart and list how you are similar to or different from the main character.	**Visit the Library!** Select a book that you can read with a partner. Create a ten-question quiz that can be answered by reading the story. Quiz your partner.	**Visit the Library!** Select a fiction book and review the illustrations. Write your opinion of the illustrations: "I think the illustrations are . . ."	**Visit the Library!** Select a book of your choice. Ask yourself if the author is qualified to write this book. Give two reasons why you think the way you do.

February *(cont.)*

Monday	Tuesday	Wednesday	Thurdsday	Friday
Visit the Library! Select and read a nonfiction book. Record five important details you noticed in the text. Explain why you think they are important.	Revisit any book you have read. Draw and complete a four-panel (boxes) comic strip showing four events that happened in your book. Write a sentence about each picture.	**Visit the Library!** Select a book you are comfortable reading. Write to the author about why you think this book does or does not appeal to your age group or grade.	**Visit the Library!** Choose a book about a topic that interests you. Pretend that you are a student from the 1800s. Explain how you might react to this book if you had read it then	Revisit a fiction book or choose a new book to read. Explain what you think could happen to the main character after the end of the book. Think of it as a sequel.
Visit the Library! Select a book of your choice. Write out the title of the text decoratively. Write a phrase for each letter in the title, using details from the text.	Look through a dictionary. Find and write the meaning of the word *research*. What is your opinion of doing research? Explain why you feel the way you do.	**Visit the Library!** Select a book of your choice. Do research on any topic mentioned in the text. Share your research with a friend or teacher.	Revisit any favorite book or use a book you are currently reading. Rewrite and defend this statement: "This book should be read by anyone who hates reading because . . . ."	Revisit any book you have read this month. Scan the text and briefly summarize it, including the main idea and four supporting details.

Notes

March

Monday	Tuesday	Wednesday	Thursday	Friday
Visit the Library! Select a book related to science. Rewrite and complete this sentence: "This book helped me to . . . ."	Choose a challenging word from the science text you chose Monday. Illustrate what the word means to you and write a caption for the picture using a meaning-loaded sentence.	**Visit the Library!** Select a book by its cover. Preview the text and pictures. Write a prediction based on your preview. Read the text and check your prediction for accuracy.	Revisit a familiar text. Choose a paragraph that you enjoy reading. Write how this paragraph is an example of good writing. Explain why you think the way you do.	Switch journals with a partner. Read the entries of this week and comment on each. State whether you learned something new or agree with the entries. Be constructive in your responses.
Visit the Library! Select a book connecting to a topic in class. Write the MOST important word, phrase, idea, or illustration you find in the text. Explain your reasoning.	Revisit the text relating to a classroom topic. Imagine you were to give a class presentation on the topic. What important facts and ideas would you include?	**Visit the Library!** Select an historical nonfiction text. Rewrite and complete this sentence: "I think the author wrote this book because . . . ."	Revisit a fiction book you have read. Choose an event that took place and compare it to a situation in your own life. Use specific details from the text to show how they compare.	**Visit the Library!** Select a poem. Read the poem twice and decide what action or further reading this poem inspires. Write what you might do now after reading the poem.
Visit the Library! Select a book about any country that interests you. Imagine you are a tour guide for this place. What might you say to the tourists? Use details to support your answer.	Revisit the text you selected on a country. Choose a paragraph of interest to you. Why do you think the author included this paragraph in the text? Explain why you think the way you do.	**Visit the Library!** Select any nonfiction text. What information should NOT be included in a summary of the text? Why do you think the way you do?	Choose a fiction book you have not read before. What characteristics of the text make it realistic or unrealistic? Use details to support your answer.	Reflect on your reading experience this week. Connect the reading to yourself, another text, and to your world.

March (cont.)

Monday	Tuesday	Wednesday	Thurdsday	Friday
Visit the Library! Select any book to read. Decide what genre this book belongs in. Rewrite and complete this sentence: "The genre of this book is _____ because it has . . ."	Revisit the book you chose on Monday. Choose a graphic organizer to sequence the events as they took place in the story. Draw and complete the organizer.	Reflect on your Tuesday entry. Using graphic organizer you completed, write a summary of the text.	Switch journals with a partner. Respond to five entries. Tell your partner what you liked or agreed witn.	Revisit any textbook you are using now. Write the aspects of nonfiction found in your text. Do you agree with the author and the aspects he or she included in the text? Explain why you think the way you do.
Visit the Library! Select any nonfiction text. Answer the Five W's—who, what, when, where, and why. Write information from the text that supports your answers.	**Visit the Library!** Select a biography. Read the text and decide what important issue or problem it makes you think of.	Revisit your journal response from Tuesday. Draw a picture for each of the Five W's you answered. Do the illustrations support your answers?	Use a dictionary to find the meaning of the word *proverb*. Can you think of a proverb used in your everyday life? Write your proverb and draw a picture of what it might look like.	Revisit any book you have read this month. Scan the text and briefly summarize the story.
		Notes		

April

Monday	Tuesday	Wednesday	Thursday	Friday
Visit the Library! Select a fiction book that will keep your interest. Review one character's actions. What do these actions say about what kind of person the character is?	Revisit your book choice from Monday. Analyze and list what you like and don't like about the character.	Continue to analyze the text from your Monday book choice. Choose a key word or phrase. What do these words tell you about the craft of writing?	Revisit your text and your journal response. How can you use what you have learned about the craft of writing?	Reflect on your reading experience yesterday. Rewrite and complete this sentence: "You can tell from this text that the author thinks . . ."
Visit the Library! Select a nonfiction book of your choice. Locate paragraph two. Write and complete this sentence: "The ideas in paragraph two are arranged to show . . ."	Using Monday's text, write an additional sentence to the first paragraph that supports the topic (main idea) sentence.	**Visit the Library!** Select a book about spring. Choose a phrase to quote. What is your initial reaction to this phrase?	**Visit the Library!** Select an additional or new resource about spring. Write one fact and one opinion found in the text.	Revisit the text chosen Wednesday or Thursday. Write one new fact and opinion that could be added to paragraph one.
Visit the Library! Select a fiction book of your choice. Quote at least five passages of good description and good dialogue and explain the purpose of each.	Revisit a familiar book of your choice. Create a list of objects mentioned. Classify selected objects as living and nonliving. Use a chart or table for organization.	**Visit the Library!** Select a book that you can read with a partner. Discuss and write in your journal what you think the author's beliefs are.	**Visit the Library!** Select a book. Write down the author's purpose (reason) for writing this book. Use details to support your thoughts and opinions.r.	Use a dictionary to look up the word *metaphor*. Write the definition and provide at least one example where an author has used a metaphor in his or her writing.

April *(cont.)*

Monday	Tuesday	Wednesday	Thurdsday	Friday
Visit the Library! Select and read a book. A *metaphor* is a literary device that describes an object not literally related. Write at least one metaphor used in the text.	Revisit a fiction text you have read. Move the main character to a new setting and explain what will happen. Be sure to describe your new setting as an author would.	**Visit the Library!** Select a nonfiction book about an unfamiliar topic. Draw a KWL chart and complete the chart before, during, and after your reading experience.	Revisit your KWL chart from Wednesday. Was the author able to answer your questions? If yes, explain. If no, what other resources could you use to find answers to the topic?	Revisit your text. Imagine you are writing a letter to the author. What two questions not already answered in the text would you ask him or her?
Visit the Library! Select a fiction book. Preview the cover and read the first page. Predict what could happen next. Continue reading. Was your prediction accurate?	Revisit your fiction book from Monday. Analyze the text and select the parts of the story that were the funniest or happiest.	**Visit the Library!** Select a fiction book. Read and identify a character that is similar to you in personality. Use details to compare your traits.	**Visit the Library!** Revisit or choose any book about spring. Write lyrics to a popular tune that explain the main idea and details in the text.	Revisit any book you have read this month. Scan the text and briefly summarize the story.
		Notes		

May

Monday	Tuesday	Wednesday	Thursday	Friday
Visit the Library! Select a non-fiction text. Analyze the text and list all the elements of nonfiction you find.	Revisit your text from Monday. Make a connection between the text and outside experiences and knowledge.	Select a nonfiction text about animals. Why do you think the author included paragraph two? Use information from the text to support your answer.	Revisit Wednesday's text. What does this text tell us about animal habitats? Use evidence from the text to support your answer. the way you you do.	Imagine you are going to give a talk to your class about an animal you studied this week. Using information from the text, write two important ideas that you would use in your speech.
Visit the Library! Select a book that interests you. Make a prediction based on the cover and text. What might you learn?	Revisit your text from Monday. Choose a challenging word to investigate. Explain what this word means in the story.	Visualize your vocabulary word. Draw what the word looks like and write a caption using the meaning.	Revisit any text you are familiar with. Analyze the author's craft of using *like* or *as* in a *simile*. Choose a simile and explain how the author used it.	Using a previously read text, make a graphic organizer to outline the main idea in paragraph/page one.
Revisit a current textbook you are reading. Write two facts that the author included showing that this topic is important.	**Visit the Library!** Choose a nonfiction text. Find one fact and one opinion. List the page numbers where you found each.	Revisit a previously read text. Explain how another concept or event or situation is similar to one in this text. Use details to support your answer.	**Visit the Library!** Select a science book. Write five facts learned and draw a picture for each. Use specific details from the text to support your answer.	Using your facts learned on Thursday, write a brief summary about the text. Use evidence from the text to support your answer.

May *(cont.)*

Monday	Tuesday	Wednesday	Thursday	Friday
Visit the Library! Choose a text on a current or historical person. Write and complete this sentence: "You can tell from this text that the author thinks . . ." Use the text to support your response.	Revisit your book from Monday. Create a speech about the main person/topic in your text. Use details to support your answers.	If the author of your text added another paragraph to the end of the story, what would it most likely describe or tell about? Use evidence from the text to support your answer.	Choose a graphic organizer to compare and contrast your current/historical person to yourself. Draw and complete the organizer with evidence from the text.	Using information from your Monday book choice, explain why the writer uses the words he or she does. Use details to support your critical stance.
Visit the Library! Choose a text familiar to you. Choose a graphic organizer to compare and contrast two items mentioned in the text. Draw and complete the organizer.	Revisit a nonfiction text. Review the aspects of nonfiction found. Choose one and explain why it is important to the text. Use specific details to support your answer.	**Visit the Library!** or Any Text at Your Desk! *Topic:* Memorial Day Write and complete this sentence: "You can tell from the passage that the author thinks . . ."	Reflect on the texts you have read about Memorial Day. What is the lesson learned from each? Use details as support when revisiting the texts	Revisit any book you have read this month. Scan the text and briefly summarize the story.
		Notes		

June

Monday	Tuesday	Wednesday	Thursday	Friday
Visit the Library! Select a fiction book to read. Write down the lesson or theme of the story.	Revisit the fiction book you chose. Describe a place you have visited that is like the setting of this story. Use details to support your answer.	Using your book choice from Monday, write a telephone conversation between two characters.r.	**Visit the Library!** Choose a picture book. Connect and decide if you know someone like the main character. List how they are alike or similar.	Revisit your fiction book. Choose a character and write five questions from his/her point of view.
Visit the Library! Select a fiction book that is unfamiliar to you. List five words in the story that are new to you. Predict why the author chose these words.	Revisit your fiction text. Review the aspects/elements of fiction found. Choose one and explain why it is important to the text.	**Visit the Library!** Select a fiction book. Read and decide if you would rather live where the story takes place or where you live now. Explain why.	Revisit the fiction book from Wednesday. Choose an important event from the text. Using details from the story, explain why you think this specific event occurred.	Revisit a fiction book you have read this month. What would happen if you added a new character to the story? Use evidence from the text to support your answer.
Visit the Library! Select a fiction book to read in an unusual place. Draw two scenes from the story, including captions to explain what is happening.	Revisit and read a fiction book that is familiar to you. Write a letter to the main character from one of the minor characters.	**Visit the Library!** Select a book that you can read with a partner. Create a ten-question quiz that can be answered by reading the story. Quiz your partner.	Revisit a favorite book. Analyze the main character and connect to someone you know that is like the main character. Draw a Venn diagram showing how they are alike and different.	**Visit the Library!** Select a fiction book of your choice. Rewrite and complete this sentence: "The character can BEST be described as ____." Give specific details for support.

June *(cont.)*

Monday	Tuesday	Wednesday	Thurdsday	Friday
Visit the Library! Select and read a fiction book. Take a critical stance and write a commercial telling why someone should read this book. Draw pictures if needed.	**Visit the Library!** Select a text that is familiar to you. Choose and draw a graphic organizer that you can use to sequence the events of the story. Use details to support your answers.	**Visit the Library!** Share a fiction book with four friends. Discuss all the story elements you find. Write a summary of your reading experience with your "book club."	**Visit the Library!** Choose a book by a favorite fiction writer. Write a letter to the author and explain your reaction to the book. Use details from the text to support your initial reaction.	Revisit a fiction book or choose a new book to read. Explain how the main character solved his or her problem. Give specific information from the story to support your answer.
Visit the Library! Select a fiction book. Review how this book is organized. List what you noticed about the structure of the text. Is this structure helpful to you?	Revisit a fiction book choice from this month. Pretend you are one of the characters and write a diary or journal entry about what happened to you in today's reading.	**Visit the Library!** Select a fiction book. Tell why this story seems realistic or unrealistic to you. Use details from the text to support your statements.	Revisit your book choices from Monday and Wednesday. Compare the main characters from each book. Would the two get along? Explain why or why not.	Revisit any book you have read this month. Scan the text and briefly tell how two characters are alike or different. Be sure to give specific information to support your answer.

Notes

July

Monday	Tuesday	Wednesday	Thursday	Friday
Visit the Library or Bookstore! Select a book that will keep your interest. Write and complete this sentence: "The title of this book says to me . . . ."	Using Monday's text, write and complete this sentence: "Another title for this book could be . . . ."	Using Monday's text, write and complete this sentence: "I think the author wrote this book . . . ."	Using Monday's text, write and complete this sentence: "This book reminds me of another book I have read. That book is . . . ."	Using Monday's text, write and complete this sentence: "If I could talk to one of the characters, I would (ask or say) . . . ."
Visit the Library! Select a favorite book to read. Write and complete this sentence: "When I read this book, I feel . . . ."	Using Monday's text, write and complete this sentence: "The setting of this story is important because . . . ."	Using Monday's text, write and complete this sentence: "I think the illustrations are . . . ."	Using Monday's text, write and complete this sentence: "If I could be any character in this book, I would be _____ because . . . ."	Using Monday's text, write and complete this sentence: "This book makes me want to . . . ."
Visit the Library! Select a fiction book you can read for the week. Write and complete this sentence: "Another title for this book could be . . . ."	Using Monday's text, write and complete this sentence: "I like this part of the story because . . . ."	Using Monday's text, write and complete this sentence: "This (person, place, time) reminds me of _____ because . . . ."	Using Monday's text, write and complete this sentence: "What I want to remember about this book is . . . ."	Using Monday's text, write and complete this sentence: "I thought this book was _____ (realistic/unrealistic) because . . . ."

July *(cont.)*

Monday	Tuesday	Wednesday	Thurdsday	Friday
Visit the Library! Select a fiction book to read that you are comfortable with. Write and complete this sentence: "I predict/infer that I will read about . . ."	Revisit the book you chose Monday. Write and complete this sentence: "I noticed that the author . . ."	Using Monday's text and complete this sentence: "The most exciting part of this book was . . ."	Using Monday's text, write and complete this sentence: "If I were _____, a character in the book, I would . . ."	Using Monday's text, write and complete this sentence: "This book helped me to . . ."
Visit the Library! Select a biography. Write and complete this sentence: "This book makes me think about . . ."	Using Monday's text, write and complete this sentence: "A question that I have about this book is _____ because . . ."	Using Monday's text, write and complete this sentence: "This [person, place, event] reminds me of _____ because . . ."	Using Monday's text, write and complete this sentence: "The big ideas in this book are . . ."	Using Monday's text, write and complete this sentence: "I'd like to read another book by this author/publisher because . . ."
		Notes		

August

Monday	Tuesday	Wednesday	Thurdsday	Friday
Visit the Library! Choose a book from your summer reading list or other book lists to enjoy for the month. Read and decide what the theme of the book is. Use details to support your answer.	Using your monthly book choice, write a prediction of what will happen next. Draw a picture to match your prediction.	Revisit your monthly book choice. Choose a character or event and write a prediction of what would happen if . . . . Complete the statement, using what has been read to support your answer.	Using your monthly book choice, draw and complete a Venn diagram to compare and contrast a character to yourself.	Using your monthly book choice, write how the characters are feeling. Use details to support your answers.
Revisit your book for this month. Reflect . . . Do you like the characters? Explain why or why not, using details to support your critical stance/opinion.	Using your monthly book choice, describe the setting, using your five senses.	Using your monthly book choice, write about three places you know that are like the setting of your book.	Using your monthly book choice, analyze why the characters act the way they do. Use evidence from the text to support your answer.	Using your monthly book choice and your reading response from Thursday, decide how you would have handled the situation differently.
Revisit your book for this month. Write and complete this sentence: "The title of this book says to me . . . "	Using your monthly book choice, write what parts of the story have been sad or upsetting. Use details to support your answer.	Using your monthly book choice, record any details from the text that make you think this story could happen in real life.	Using your monthly book choice, analyze the author's craft. Investigate *analogy*. An *analogy* shows partial similarities between two things. In your journal, make an analogy using, "It's like . . . "	Using your monthly book choice, take a critical stance and explain what your opinion is of this text so far. Use details to support your answer.

August *(cont.)*

Monday	Tuesday	Wednesday	Thurdsday	Friday
Continue reading your book choice for this month. Reflect on your choice of this book to read. Write in your journal what your purpose was and is for reading this book	Revisit your monthly book choice. What questions do you have relating to the text? Where might you find your answers?	Using your monthly book choice, draw and complete a sequence chain highlighting the main events from the story.	Using your monthly book choice, decide how your characters have changed while reading this book. Record the actions or character's "growth" that has occurred so far.	Using your monthly book choice, explain what the main character would be LEAST likely to do, and explain why you think the way you do.
Revisit your book choice for this month. Choose five words from the text. Write five synonyms and five antonyms for each word.	Using your monthly book choice, choose two words to illustrate. Write a "meaning"-ful caption for each word.	Using your monthly book choice, choose singular nouns from the text. Change these words to plural form. Write each new word in a sentence that could be added to the text.	Using your monthly book choice, choose five present tense verbs. Add the –ed ending (if it is appropriate) to each. Write each word in a sentence that can be added to the book.	Using your monthly book choice, create a different ending to the text you have completed.
		Notes		

Month of _____

Monday	Tuesday	Wednesday	Thurdsday	Friday

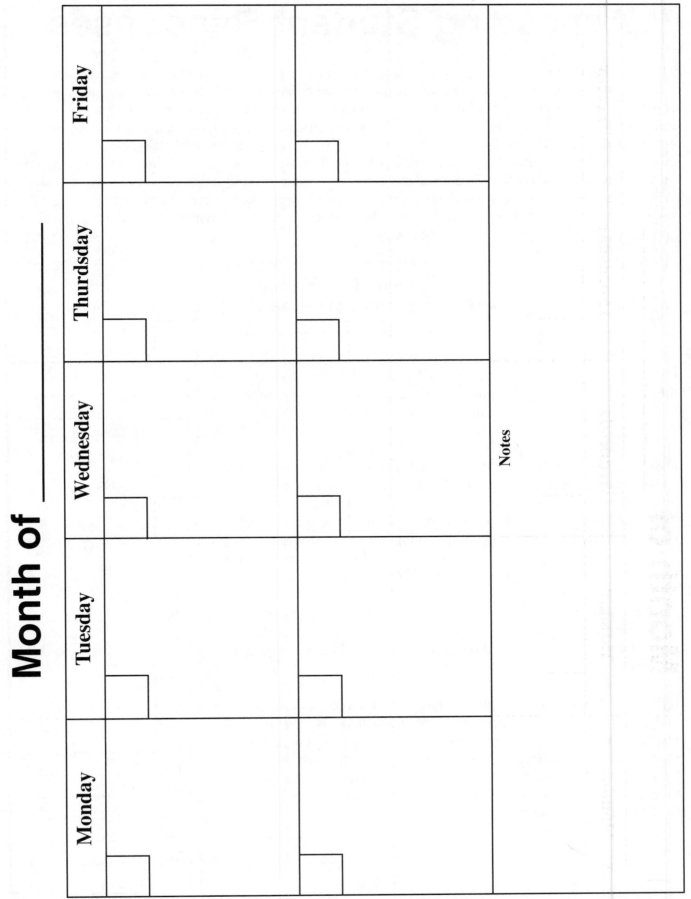

Month of _____

Monday	Tuesday	Wednesday	Thurdsday	Friday

Notes

Chapter 9

Assessing Student Responses

This independent reading response program acts as an alternative assessment to running records or other language arts assessments. Student responses can be assessed daily, weekly, or monthly, depending on the teacher. It is important that students are provided with feedback as soon as possible. Realistically, it is challenging to respond to 20 or more journals each day—even each week or month— but as good teachers know, it can and will be done. To ease the stress of responding, universal feedback stickers or labels can be created to place right inside the journal. Any label-maker program on the computer can do this. Create various sheets of responses critiquing positively on the journal. When time is limited, simply use the programmed label appropriate for the students and/or journal responses to stick inside the journal. Though the response is not hand written, the students will still appreciate the effort made to review their work.

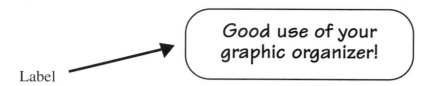

Label → Good use of your graphic organizer!

On a daily basis, review journals to ensure students are responding and are keeping organized within their folders. If certain students are off track, leave a sticky note on their folders or in their journals with reminders on how to complete the activity daily.

On a weekly basis, it is possible to check five to eight journals for responses and organization. Provide feedback on how effective their responses are, based on the rubric. Try to end with a positive remark on the responses. After every ten weeks, encourage students to share their journals with a classmate. During the shared experience, partners can respond to the journal responses, stating what they enjoyed, disliked, or connected with. Each journal should have at least ten peer responses for a grade by the end of the year.

On a monthly basis, review each folder for responses and organization. Again, respond to those that need it and grade each, using a checkmark scale. Grades can be recorded on the back of the folder on the grading stickers (page 66).

By the end of the year, students will have two to three journals filled with quality independent responses. Encourage students to revisit their response journals from the beginning of the year and to compare that level of response with their current journal. They are often proud of the difference and growth they have made in analyzing text. An average of the monthly grades can be taken and used as part of the final language arts grade.

Take the Lead and READ
Grade
Scale:
✓ + Excellent
✓ Good
✓ – Poor
Month:
Aug: _____
Sept: _____
Oct:_____
Nov: _____
Dec:_____
Jan: _____
Feb:_____
Mar: _____
Apr:_____
May: _____
Jun: _____
Jul: _____
Average: _____

Independent Reading
Folder Sticker

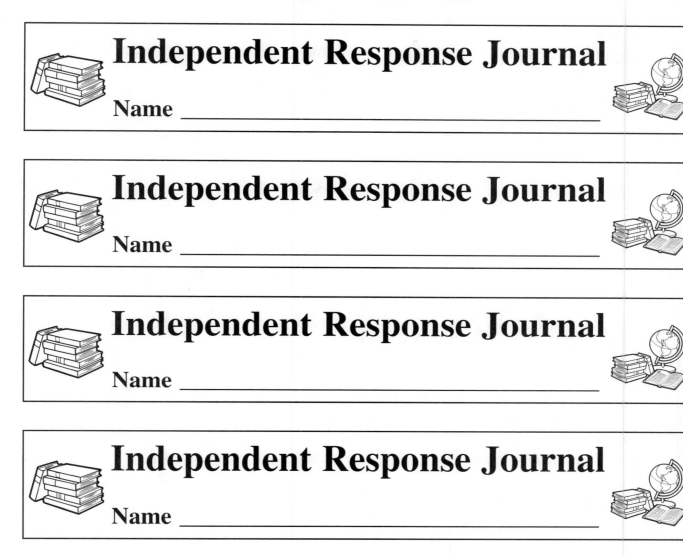

Independent Response Journal

Name _____

Independent Response Journal

Name _____

Independent Response Journal

Name _____

Independent Response Journal

Name _____

Independent Response Journal

Name _____

Independent Response Journal

Name _____

Independent Reading
Assessment Sticker

Grade	Grade	Grade
Scale: ✓ + Excellent ✓ Good ✓ − Poor Month: Aug: _____ Sept: _____ Oct:_____ Nov: _____ Dec:_____ Jan: _____ Feb:_____ Mar: _____ Apr:_____ May: _____ Jun: _____ Jul: _____ Average: _____	Scale: ✓ + Excellent ✓ Good ✓ − Poor Month: Aug: _____ Sept: _____ Oct:_____ Nov: _____ Dec:_____ Jan: _____ Feb:_____ Mar: _____ Apr:_____ May: _____ Jun: _____ Jul: _____ Average: _____	Scale: ✓ + Excellent ✓ Good ✓ − Poor Month: Aug: _____ Sept: _____ Oct:_____ Nov: _____ Dec:_____ Jan: _____ Feb:_____ Mar: _____ Apr:_____ May: _____ Jun: _____ Jul: _____ Average: _____
Grade	Grade	Grade
Scale: ✓ + Excellent ✓ Good ✓ − Poor Month: Aug: _____ Sept: _____ Oct:_____ Nov: _____ Dec:_____ Jan: _____ Feb:_____ Mar: _____ Apr:_____ May: _____ Jun: _____ Jul: _____ Average: _____	Scale: ✓ + Excellent ✓ Good ✓ − Poor Month: Aug: _____ Sept: _____ Oct:_____ Nov: _____ Dec:_____ Jan: _____ Feb:_____ Mar: _____ Apr:_____ May: _____ Jun: _____ Jul: _____ Average: _____	Scale: ✓ + Excellent ✓ Good ✓ − Poor Month: Aug: _____ Sept: _____ Oct:_____ Nov: _____ Dec:_____ Jan: _____ Feb:_____ Mar: _____ Apr:_____ May: _____ Jun: _____ Jul: _____ Average: _____

My Reading Log

Title and Author (include illustrator)	Rating (outstanding, good, fair, poor)

Open-Ended Response Scoring Rubric

	Scoring Rubric *
2	Response presents a reasonable explanation that answers the question. Response uses specific, relevant details from the passage as support.
1	Response presents a mostly reasonable explanation that answers the question. Response uses general information as support, rather than details from the passage.
0	Response presents an unreasonable explanation that does not answer the question. The response is vague.

	Scoring Rubric *
2	Response presents a reasonable explanation that answers the question. Response uses specific, relevant details from the passage as support.
1	Response presents a mostly reasonable explanation that answers the question. Response uses general information as support, rather than details from the passage.
0	Response presents an unreasonable explanation that does not answer the question. The response is vague.

* *Rubric developed by the National Assessment Governing Board Reading Framework for the National Assessment of Educational Progress.*

Sentence Leads for Reading Response Journals

This (*character, place, event*) reminds me of _____ because . . .

I like/dislike this book because . . .

I like/dislike this part of the book because . . .

This situation reminds me of something that happened in my own life.

The character I (*like best, admire, dislike the most*) is _____ because . . .

I like this part of the story because . . .

The setting of this story is important because . . .

This book makes me think about (*an important social issue, a problem, and so on*) . . .

A question that I have about this book is _____ because . . .

When I read this book I felt . . .

If I were this character, I would . . .

(*Character*) reminds me of (*myself, a friend, a family member*) because . . .

If I could talk to one of the book's characters I would (*ask or say*) . . .

I predict that _____ because . . .

This (*phrase, sentence, paragraph*) is an example of good writing because . . .

This (*person, place, time*) reminds me of . . .

I admire (*character*) because . . .

I did not understand the part of the story when . . .

This book reminds me of another book I have read . . .

The most exciting part of the book was . . .

The big ideas in this book were . . . .

Some important details I noticed were _____. They were important because . . .

My favorite part of the book was . . .

I think the author wrote this book to . . .

I think the author wanted me to learn . . .

I found this book hard to follow when . . .

The author got me interested when . . .

Sentence Leads for Reading Response Journals (cont.)

The book is really about . . .
After the book ends, I predict . . .
I am like or different from (character) . . .
I learned . . .
This book makes me want to (action, further reading) . . .
After reading the first (paragraph, page, chapter) of this book I felt . . .
The title of this book says to me . . .
Another title for this book could be . . .
If I could be any character in this book, I would be _____ because . . .
What I want to remember about this book is . . .
I'd like to read another book by this author because . . .
The most important (word, phrase, idea, illustration) in this book is . . .
As compared to other books (by this author, on the same topic), I think this book is . . .
My opinion of this book is . . .
My feelings/opinion about the book changed when . . .
This book is an effective piece of writing because . . .
I thought this book was (realistic, unrealistic) because . . .
I question the accuracy of . . .
The genre of this book is _____ because it has (characteristics and aspects of / fiction/nonfiction) . . .
I (agreed/disagreed) with the author about . . .
I think the illustrations . . .
I noticed that the author . . .
If I were the author, I would have changed the part of the story when . . .
The author is qualified to write this book because . . .
To summarize the text, I would say . . .
This book helped me to . . .
If I were to add another sentence to the end it would be _____ because . . .

QAR Focus-Questions Bookmark

I Question . . .

QAR Bookmark

Right There
Who?
What?
Where?
When?

Think and Search
What is meant by . . . ?
Can you describe . . . ?
What is the difference . . . ?
What is the main idea . . . ?

Author and Me
Who would you choose . . . ?
What would happen if . . . ?
How would you . . . ?
Do you know someone like . . . ?
Why . . . ?
What if . . . ?
What was the purpose . . . ?

On My Own
How could we/you . . . ?
What if . . . ?
Do you suppose that . . . ?
I wonder how . . . ?
Which is better . . . ?
Would you agree that . . . ?
Would it be better if . . . ?
What is your opinion . . . ?
Were they/you/we right to . . . ?

I Question . . .

QAR Bookmark

Right There
Who?
What?
Where?
When?

Think and Search
What is meant by . . . ?
Can you describe . . . ?
What is the difference . . . ?
What is the main idea . . . ?

Author and Me
Who would you choose . . . ?
What would happen if . . . ?
How would you . . . ?
Do you know someone like . . . ?
Why . . . ?
What if . . . ?
What was the purpose . . . ?

On My Own
How could we/you . . . ?
What if . . . ?
Do you suppose that . . . ?
I wonder how . . . ?
Which is better . . . ?
Would you agree that . . . ?
Would it be better if . . . ?
What is your opinion . . . ?
Were they/you/we right to . . . ?

Note: Photocopy this page and then cut in half. Laminating will preserve the bookmark.

Dr. Sue Deffenbaugh Bookmark

Initial Understanding

– What is your first reaction to this story? What did you think or wonder about while you were reading it?

Main Idea and Theme

– What is paragraph # _____ mainly about?
– The main idea of this article is . . .
– What question does paragraph # _____ answer?
– What is the lesson or theme of this story?

Characters, Settings, Problems, Events, Relationships, & Details in a Written Work

– According to the article, who . . . , what . . . , when . . . , how . . . , why . . . ? What information in the article supports your answer?
– In this story who . . . , what . . . , when . . . , how . . . , why . . . (setting, events, characters, solution)? What happenings, details, or information in the story support your answer?
– Using information in the story, write a BRIEF description on how _____ felt when _____.
– The character _____ can BEST be described as (friendly, sneaky, happy, careless, etc.) Give specific events or information from the story as support.
– Write a brief paragraph telling how two characters (or events) are alike or different. Be sure to give specific information from the story to support your answer.

Summary

– Briefly summarize the story or article.
– Which information should NOT be included in a summary of the story/ article?
– If you could rename this article/story, what would you call it and why? Use specific details from the story/article to support your answer.

Context Clues

– You can tell from what is said in the story that _____ means . . .
– In this story, the word _____ means . . .

Developing Interpretation

Making Connections with Experiences and Knowledge

– The situation described in _____ is MOST like . . .
– The _____ could be compared to . . .
– Today a _____ might BEST be compared to . . .
– What is a similar situation or event in our world? In our school? In our families?

Use of Structure/Organizational Patterns

– Paragraph #_____ of this story/article can be described as (a conversation, an explanation, a description, a comparison, etc.). What information in the paragraph suggests this?
– Make a graphic organizer or outline showing the most important ideas in paragraph # _____ .
– Fill in the sequence chain with the important events.
– On a Venn diagram, fill in how the _____ are similar and/or different.
– Which one of these events belongs in Box # _____?

Author's Purpose

– Why does the author include paragraph #_____ ? (to explain . . . , describe . . . , compare . . . , define . . . , etc.).
– The author mentioned _____ to (explain . . . , tell . . ., describe . . . , show . . . , etc.).
– The purpose of paragraph #_____ is to (describe . . . , give examples, solve a problem, compare . . . , etc.).

Use Evidence

– You can tell from the information in the passage that . . .
– Which of the following sentences can be supported with evidence from the passage?
– Which facts support the conclusion that . . . ?

Reprinted by permission of Dr. Sue Deffenbaugh, 10/99

Note: Copy this bookmark and fold in half.

Dr. Sue Deffenbaugh Bookmark *(cont.)*

Moving Beyond the Text

Making a Prediction Based on What Is Read

- Tell or write a brief paragraph about what PROBABLY would have happened if . . . Use information from the story/article to support your answer.

- Based on the information in the story, what will MOST LIKELY happen in the future? Use information from the story to support your answer.

- What will _____ do next? Use information from the story to support your answer.

Author's Craft
(including use of literary devices)

- A *simile* is a comparison using *as* or *like*. Choose a simile from the story/article and explain why the author used that simile.

- Why does the author emphasize . . . ? Use information from the story to support your answer.

Evaluate Explicit and Implicit Information and Themes

- You can tell from this story that the author thinks . . .

- Find one fact and one opinion in the article (or in paragraph # _____).

- Which of these is an OPINION found in the article?

- Would the author PROBABLY agree that . . . ? Use information from the article to support your answer.

- With which of the following statements would the author probably agree? Use information from the story to support your answer.

Using Relevant Information in Responding to or Extending a Written Work

- Choose the part of the story that you think was MOST important. Use details from the story to explain why you chose that part.

- Imagine you are writing a letter to the author of this article. Write two questions not already answered in the article that you will ask the author.

- Imagine that you are giving a talk to your class about . . . . Using information from the article, write two ideas that you would use in your speech.

- Using information from the story, write an imaginary journal page of (*character*) when . . . (*event*).

- If the author added another sentence at the end of this story, what might it be? Use information from the story to support your answer.

- Which one of these sentences would BEST fit with the ideas in paragraph #_____?

Awareness of Values, Customs, Ethics, and Beliefs in a Written Work

- How can you tell that (*a particular character or the author*) cares about . . . ? Use information from the story/article to support your answer.

- Which one of the following would PROBABLY be the most important thing (*a particular character or the author*) cares about? Use information from the story/article to support your answer.

- According to the passage, what human characteristics seemed to be highly valued by . . . ? Use information from the article to support your answer.

Reprinted by permission of Dr. Sue Deffenbaugh, 10/99

Note : *Copy this bookmark and fold in half.*

T-Chart

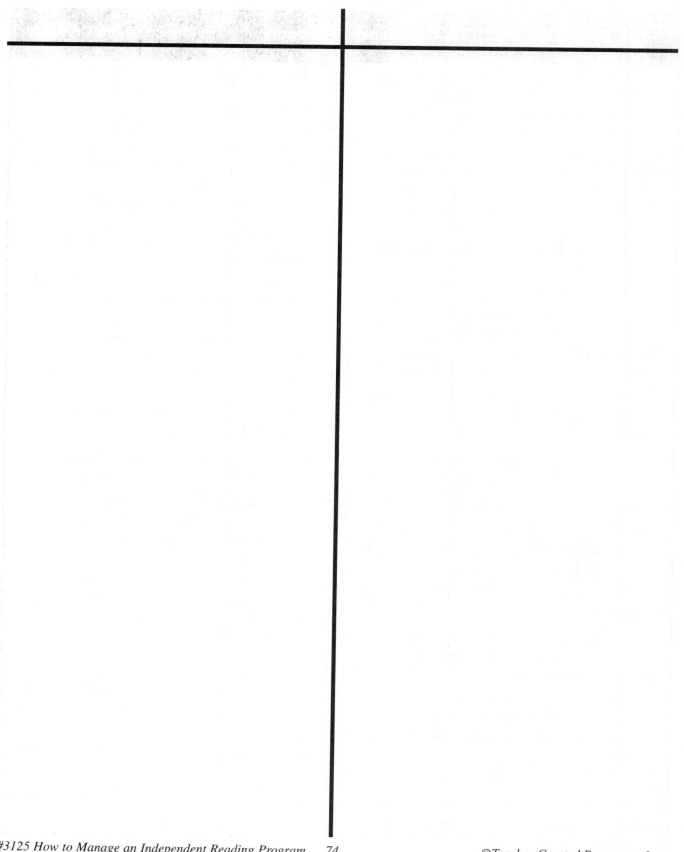

Prediction Organizer

Prediction	Evidence to Support	Evidence to the Contrary

Venn Diagram

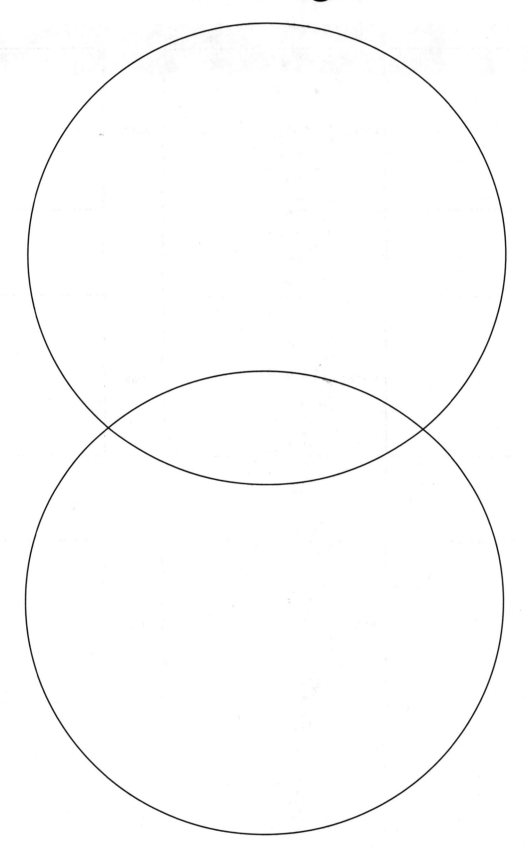

Sequence Chain

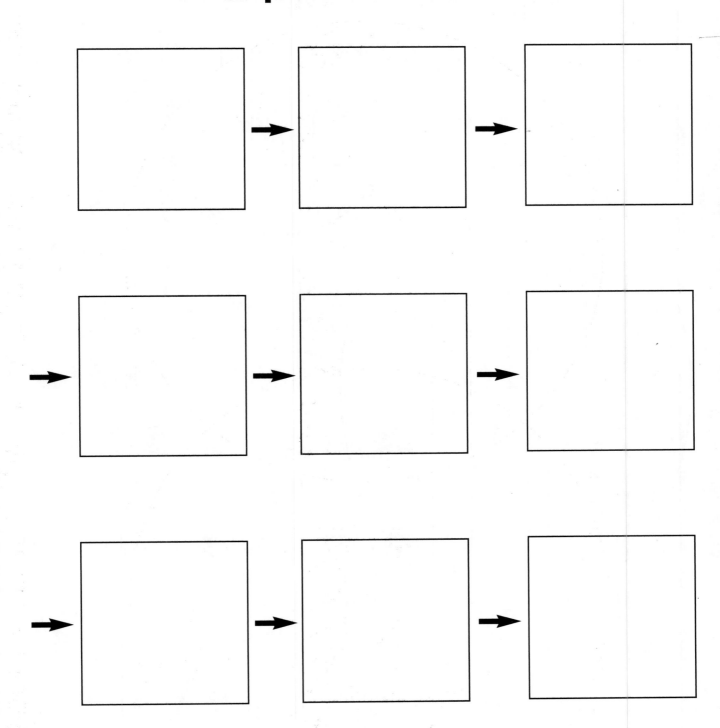

Main Idea/Detail Organizer

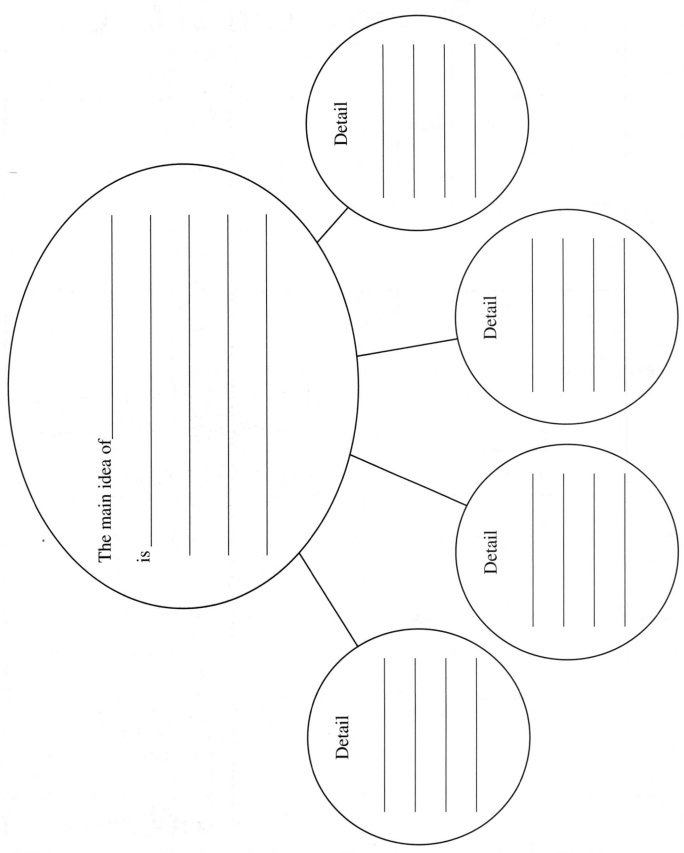

Cause and Effect Map/
Problem and Solution Map

Cause   **Effect**

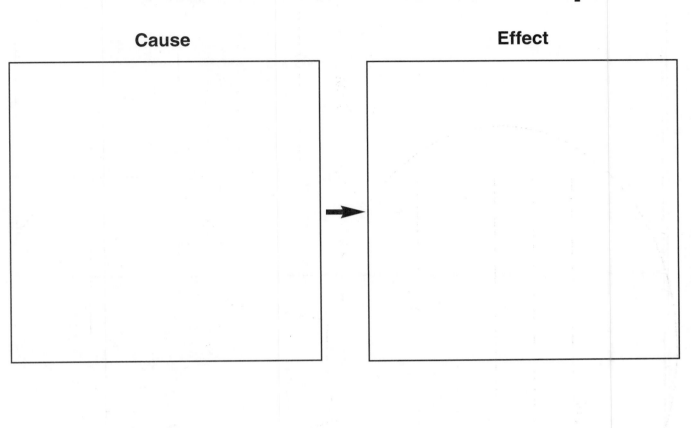

Problem   **Solution**

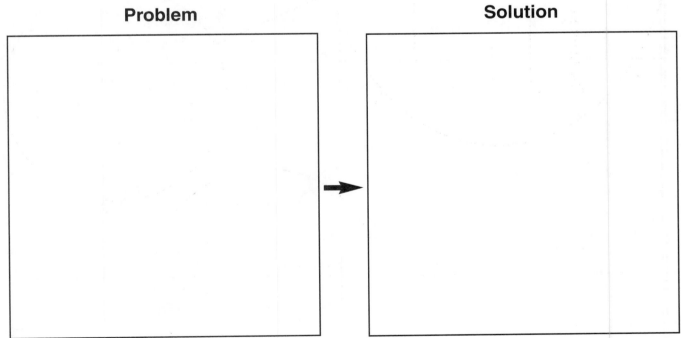

Time Order Timeline

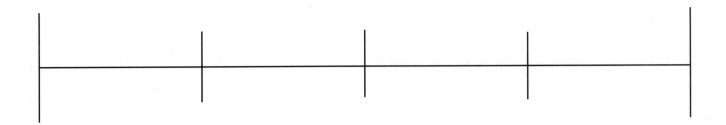

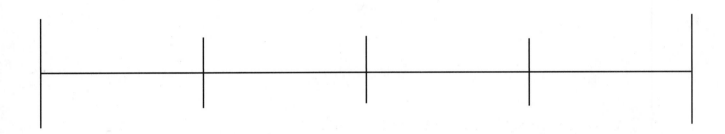

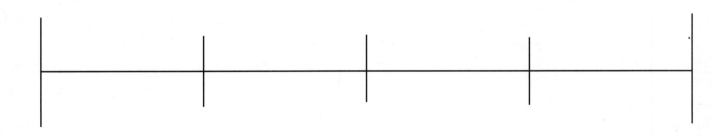